D1372356

HOW
NATURE
WORKS

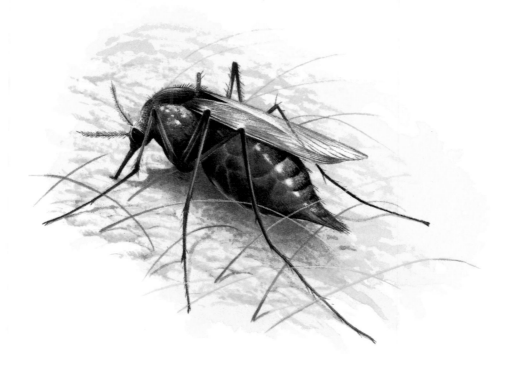

No part of this publication may be reproduced in whole or in part,
or stored in a retrieval system, or transmitted in any form
or by any means, electronic, mechanical, photocopying, recording,
or otherwise, without written permission of the publisher.
For information regarding permission,
write to Larousse Kingfisher Chambers Inc.,
95 Madison Avenue,
New York, NY 10016.

ISBN 0-439-17318-3

Copyright © 1992 by Grisewood and Dempsey Limited. All rights reserved.
Published by Scholastic Inc., 555 Broadway, New York, NY 10012,
by arrangement with Larousse Kingfisher Chambers Inc.
SCHOLASTIC and associated logos are trademarks
and/or registered trademarks of Scholastic Inc.

12 11 10 9 8 7 6 5 4   3 4 5/0

Printed in the U.S.A.   14
First Scholastic printing, March 2000

Editor: Stuart Cooper
Design: David West Children's Book Design and Branka Surla

HOW
NATURE
WORKS

STEVE PARKER

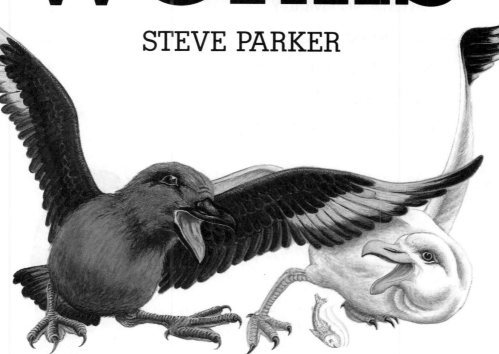

SCHOLASTIC INC.

New York Toronto London Auckland Sydney
Mexico City New Delhi Hong Kong

CONTENTS

RESPIRATION AND CIRCULATION

GROWING AND MOVING

THE SENSES

NERVES, BRAINS, AND BEHAVIOR

REPRODUCTION

SOCIALIZING

THE WEB OF NATURE

INTRODUCTION

In the summer sunshine a bumblebee alights on a flower. Its tongue laps up the sweet nectar. The bee digests some of the nectar for its own energy needs and takes the rest back to the nest to feed the growing grubs. As it feeds, it collects a fine yellow powder—pollen grains—on its body and legs. At the next flower it visits, some of these pollen grains rub off the bee and onto the flower. Male cells in the pollen grains join with female cells in the flower's ovary. They ripen into seeds, which only start to grow if they find a suitable place with the right conditions of soil, moisture, and light.

The world of nature is intricate and fascinating, beautiful and dangerous. *How Nature Works* unravels this complex and tangled web to illustrate the basic principles of how animals, plants, and other organisms live, and how they relate to each other and their environments.

The book is divided into nine main sections, each building upon the last. "The Basics of Nature" discuss water, air, and land, and the special ways in which atoms, elements, and molecules combine to make living cells. The methods by which living things obtain energy and nutrients, and the feeding relationships involving plants, herbivores, and carnivores, are explored in "Food for Life." Obtaining oxygen, and spreading both it and nutrients through a

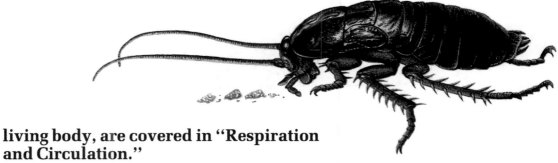

living body, are covered in "Respiration and Circulation."

Growth is an ongoing process throughout life, and the ability to move is an important animal attribute; these functions are explained in "Growing and Moving." "The Senses" describes how animals obtain information about the world around them. "Nerves, Brains, and Behavior" shows how they process this information and carry out appropriate actions. Another vital aspect of living things—how they reproduce—is covered in "Breeding and Multiplying." The interactions between animals in groups are discussed in "Socializing." The final section draws these diverse strands together into "The Web of Nature."

Many structures, processes, and relationships occur again and again in different parts of the natural world. These concepts are explained in the "Glossary," together with less familiar scientific terms.

So the next time you see a bee visit a flower, or listen to bird song, or glimpse a squirrel searching for nuts—think about the multitude of processes and connections in the living world. And, consider that nature's delicate balance is under threat. We are destroying great areas of our planet for our own ends. Hopefully we will come to our senses sooner than later; later may be too late.

THE BASICS OF NATURE

The Earth is a huge ball of rocks about 8,000 miles across. It has a mostly metal center and a thin layer of gases at its surface. It spins around once every 24 hours. And it speeds through space in orbit around its nearest star, the sun, at almost 66,600 miles per hour. Yet somehow, conditions on this planet are such that living things can survive. A flourishing natural world of plants, animals, and other organisms has existed on Earth for hundreds of millions of years.

The bodies of these living things are made from the same basic building blocks that form the rocks, water, gases, and other nonliving parts of the Earth—carbon, hydrogen, oxygen, nitrogen, and other chemical elements. Animals and plants are special because they can feed, breathe, and most importantly, breed. Most life takes place in the Earth's surface waters and in a very thin layer at the boundary between the air and the rocks. This "layer of life" is the biosphere.

EARTH THROUGH THE AGES

The Earth probably formed from a cloud of dust and gas 4.6 billion years ago. Fossils show that life forms appeared 3.5 billion years ago. For 2.5 billion years they were small and simple. Larger organisms appeared less than 1 billion years ago.

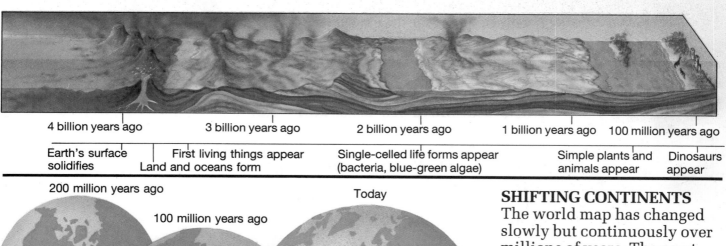

4 billion years ago	3 billion years ago	2 billion years ago	1 billion years ago	100 million years ago
Earth's surface solidifies	First living things appear / Land and oceans form	Single-celled life forms appear (bacteria, blue-green algae)	Simple plants and animals appear	Dinosaurs appear

200 million years ago

100 million years ago

Today

SHIFTING CONTINENTS

The world map has changed slowly but continuously over millions of years. The great land masses, the continents, have drifted, split, and collided, and the oceans have shrunk and widened. These movements are still happening, causing earthquakes and volcanic eruptions.

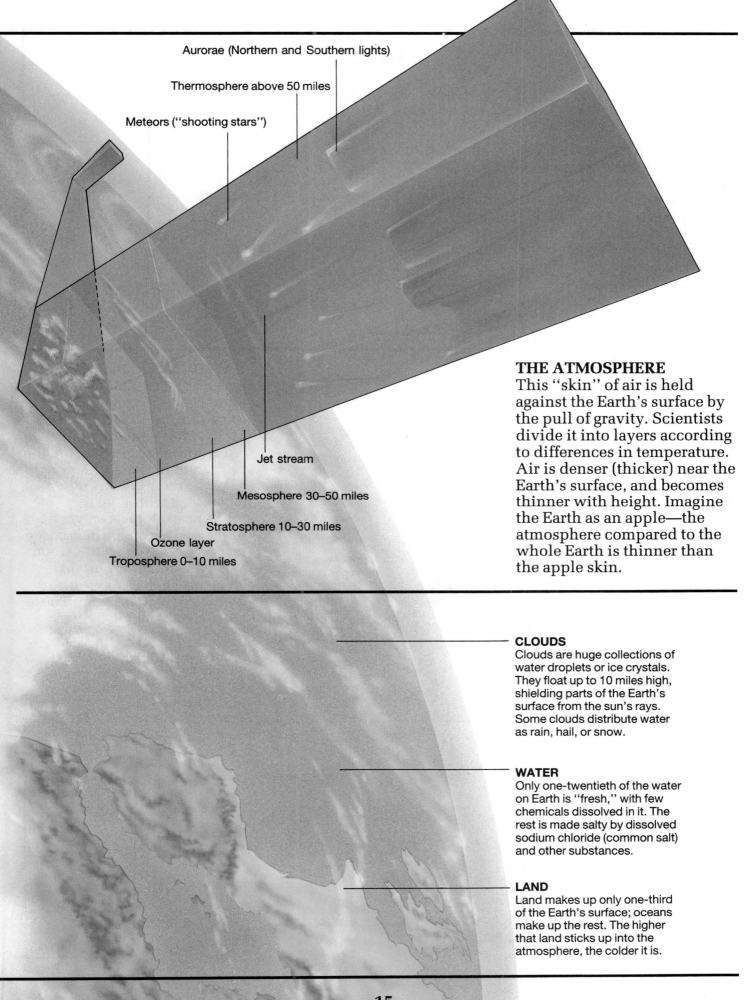

Aurorae (Northern and Southern lights)

Thermosphere above 50 miles

Meteors ("shooting stars")

Jet stream

Mesosphere 30–50 miles

Stratosphere 10–30 miles

Ozone layer

Troposphere 0–10 miles

THE ATMOSPHERE

This "skin" of air is held against the Earth's surface by the pull of gravity. Scientists divide it into layers according to differences in temperature. Air is denser (thicker) near the Earth's surface, and becomes thinner with height. Imagine the Earth as an apple—the atmosphere compared to the whole Earth is thinner than the apple skin.

CLOUDS

Clouds are huge collections of water droplets or ice crystals. They float up to 10 miles high, shielding parts of the Earth's surface from the sun's rays. Some clouds distribute water as rain, hail, or snow.

WATER

Only one-twentieth of the water on Earth is "fresh," with few chemicals dissolved in it. The rest is made salty by dissolved sodium chloride (common salt) and other substances.

LAND

Land makes up only one-third of the Earth's surface; oceans make up the rest. The higher that land sticks up into the atmosphere, the colder it is.

CHEMICALS OF LIFE

All things on Earth are made up of atoms. A single atom is too small to see, even under a powerful microscope. There are about 100 different kinds of atoms, but only 20–30 are common in living things. Atoms link together into groups called molecules. The biggest molecules are just visible under a powerful microscope. From these simple building blocks—atoms and molecules—grow dangerous germs, giant redwood trees, and great white sharks.

OXYGEN
Oxygen makes up about one-fifth of the air. Each oxygen molecule is made of two oxygen atoms. This gas is given off by plants in photosynthesis (page 28). Bubbles from pondweeds contain oxygen.

CARBON
Lumps of coal, burnt toast, the "lead" in a pencil, the diamond in a ring—these are all forms of carbon. This element's chemical adaptability makes it a central building block in living things.

NITROGEN
Nitrogen molecules are made of two nitrogen atoms. This gas makes up almost four-fifths of the air. Nitrogen gas is colorless, tasteless, and odorless, but the element is part of many important chemicals.

HYDROGEN
Made of two hydrogen atoms, these small molecules form a tiny proportion of the gases in air. But hydrogen is present in most of the molecules needed for life.

CHEMICAL ELEMENTS
Each different kind of atom is known as an element. Four of the most important elements for life are shown on the left. All atoms of an element are the same, and they are different from the atoms of any other element. It would take millions of atoms to cover a pinhead. Life on Earth is based mainly on the element carbon and a few other important elements such as oxygen, hydrogen, and nitrogen. These are present outside living things too, in the air, rocks, and soil. Other common elements in plants and animals are sulfur and phosphorus.

JOINING ELEMENTS
When atoms of different elements join, they form molecules of a new and different substance. A molecule may contain two atoms, or three, or four . . . or millions! A molecule of water consists of two hydrogen atoms and one oxygen atom. Carbon dioxide, a gas in the air, has one carbon atom and two oxygen atoms.

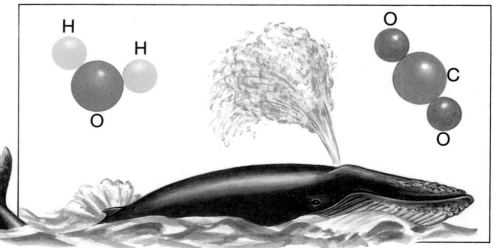

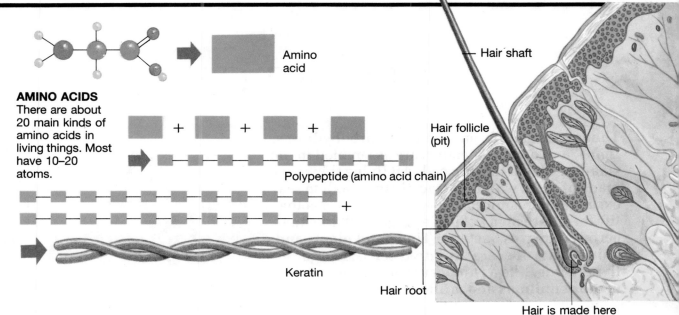

ATOMS
Atoms of carbon, hydrogen, nitrogen, oxygen, and other elements join to make an amino acid.

AMINO ACIDS
There are about 20 main kinds of amino acids in living things. Most have 10–20 atoms.

PROTEIN
Amino acids link together into chains, sheets, corkscrews, and other shapes to form a protein. This is the protein keratin.

Amino acid

Polypeptide (amino acid chain)

Keratin

Hair shaft

Hair follicle (pit)

Hair root

Hair is made here

PROTEINS

Like the bricks of a house, protein molecules make up the structural parts of a living body. The protein keratin forms the skin, fur, nails, claws, and hooves of mammals, and the protein collagen makes up bones, teeth, and cartilage. Each protein is made from strings or sheets of smaller molecules known as amino acids. Many proteins are huge molecules composed of thousands of atoms from several different elements.

Nectar in flowers, and the honey that bees make from it, contain sugar. A small sugar is glucose, $C_6H_{12}O_6$.

6 x C   12 x H   6 x O

$C_6H_{12}O_6$ (glucose sugar)

SUGARS (CARBOHYDRATES)

Sugars, the power sources of life, contain energy in the chemical links, or bonds, between their atoms. A living thing can break the bonds and use the supply of energy. Many sugar molecules joined together make starches and the plant substance called cellulose. These are all carbohydrates, containing atoms of carbon, hydrogen, and oxygen.

FATS (LIPIDS)

Lots of fat may not be healthy for humans, but fat is vital for creatures such as whales and walruses. A thick layer of fat under the skin, called blubber, helps to keep these mammals warm in the icy polar seas. There are many kinds of fats and oils, more properly called lipids, in living things. They are mostly built from repeating units of two hydrogen atoms and one carbon atom:

$$-CH_2-CH_2-CH_2-$$

Lipids contain mainly carbon and hydrogen. A thick layer of fatty blubber keeps the walrus warm in cold Arctic seas.

C   H   O

Fats can be used for protection and insulation, to build structures such as cell membranes and nerves, to control aspects of body chemistry, and broken down to provide energy.

PLANT CELLS

Thousands of different proteins, carbohydrates, lipids, and other molecules are assembled in the smallest unit of life, the cell. All living things are made of cells, which are mostly too small to see except under a microscope. The bodies of some life forms are made of just a single cell, like the germs known as bacteria. Tiny pond plants and animals have several hundred cells. A large living thing, like a rhinoceros or a pine tree, is made of millions and millions of cells.

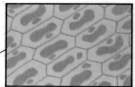

Close-up of leaf cells

INSIDE A PLANT CELL

There are several basic differences between a typical plant cell, shown here, and a typical animal cell (page 20). One difference is that a plant cell has a thick, stiff outer casing made of the substance cellulose. Another is that it has a large watery "bag" near its center called the vacuole. Plant cells also differ from animal cells in that many of them contain chloroplasts (see below). Animal cells do not have chloroplasts.

Inside, a cell is not just an unorganized jumble of bits and pieces. Its watery fluid, the cytoplasm, is divided into numerous compartments by very thin "walls" known as membranes. Collectively, these membranes make up the endoplasmic reticulum which spreads throughout the cell. Also inside the cell are several kinds of tiny structures known as organelles. Each type of organelle has a specific role in keeping the cell alive, making products for other cells to use, or dealing with the wastes produced by the cell. The membranes may separate these different activities so that they do not interfere with each other. The cell's contents may also be moved along "corridors" in the endoplasmic reticulum.

CHLOROPLAST

Like solar power stations that capture light energy and turn it into electricity, chloroplasts capture light energy and turn it into chemical energy.

Cell membrane

Vacuole membrane

Cytoplasm

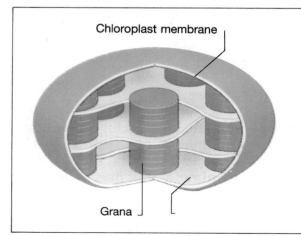

Chloroplast membrane

Grana

INSIDE A CHLOROPLAST

An average chloroplast is slightly less than one one-thousandth of an inch across. Inside are stacks of membranes known as grana. These contain the vital substance known as chlorophyll, which traps light energy during the process of photosynthesis (page 28). Some plant cells have hundreds of chloroplasts.

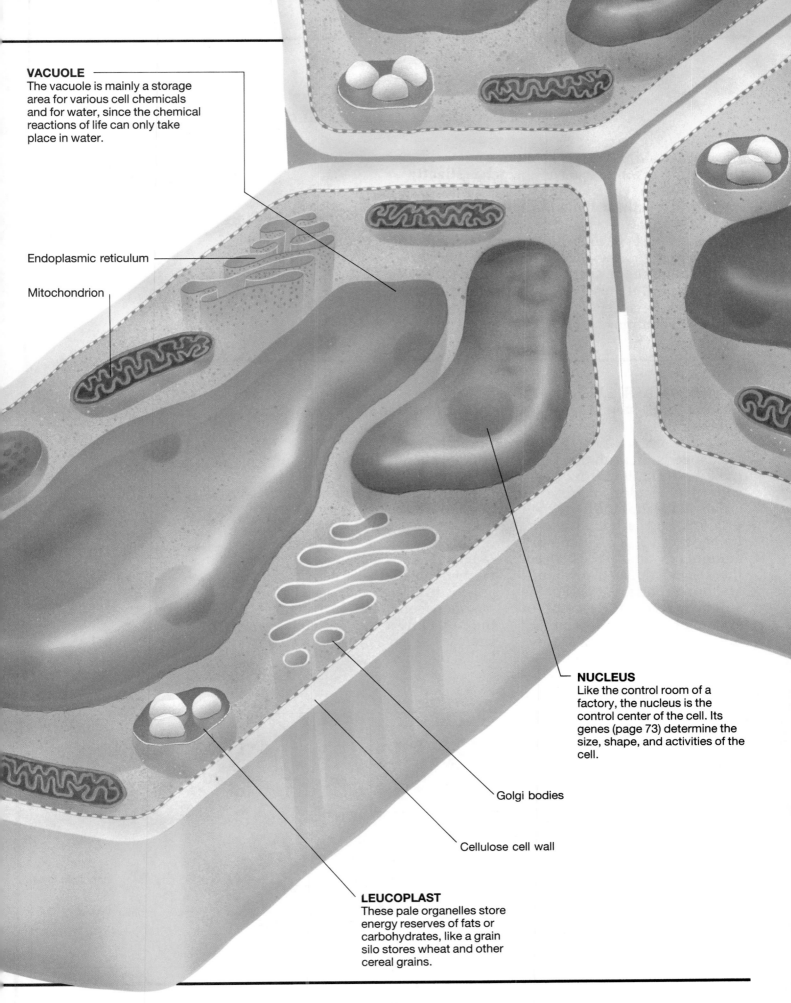

VACUOLE
The vacuole is mainly a storage area for various cell chemicals and for water, since the chemical reactions of life can only take place in water.

Endoplasmic reticulum

Mitochondrion

NUCLEUS
Like the control room of a factory, the nucleus is the control center of the cell. Its genes (page 73) determine the size, shape, and activities of the cell.

Golgi bodies

Cellulose cell wall

LEUCOPLAST
These pale organelles store energy reserves of fats or carbohydrates, like a grain silo stores wheat and other cereal grains.

ANIMAL CELLS

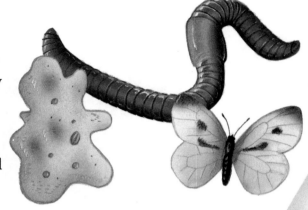

An average animal cell is about one one-thousandth of an inch across, which is slightly smaller than a typical plant cell. Its outer "skin" is a thin layer, the cell membrane. This is usually flexible so that the cell can change shape. The nucleus tends to be near the center of the cell. In a creature such as a worm or butterfly, few cells are the same shape as the "generalized" cell shown here. But most contain the same parts and organelles. Each cell is just like a microscopic industrial complex.

INSIDE AN ANIMAL CELL

The outer cell membrane of an animal cell is both its protective coat and its exchange point with the outside world. It lets in only certain molecules, such as amino acids for building proteins, and carbohydrates for energy. It also regulates the amount of water in the cell, so that the cell does not swell up and burst. The main part of the animal cell contains a complex system of microtubules and microfilaments known as the cytoskeleton, that gives the cell structure and firmness. Membranes divide regions of the cell into different compartments, and form bases for chemical reactions such as the making of proteins and the breaking down of sugars. The nucleus is wrapped in a double membrane with pores, or holes, in it. These pores let very large molecules, carrying genetic information (page 73), pass between it and the rest of the cell. Only a very few cells, such as the red cells in blood, lack a nucleus.

Cell membrane

Nucleolus

Centriole

THE CELL MEMBRANE

The main components of cell membranes are lipid molecules. There are two layers of them, back to back. Embedded in the lipid layers are much bigger molecules of various proteins, which act as entrance and exit points for sugars, amino acids, and other substances. Different proteins may act as "gateways" for different substances passing through the membrane.

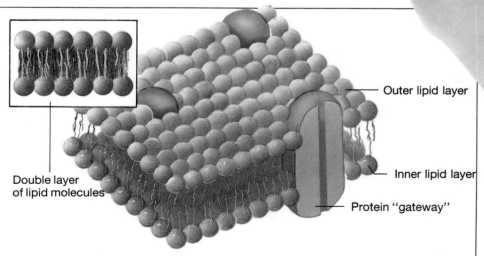

Double layer of lipid molecules

Outer lipid layer

Inner lipid layer

Protein "gateway"

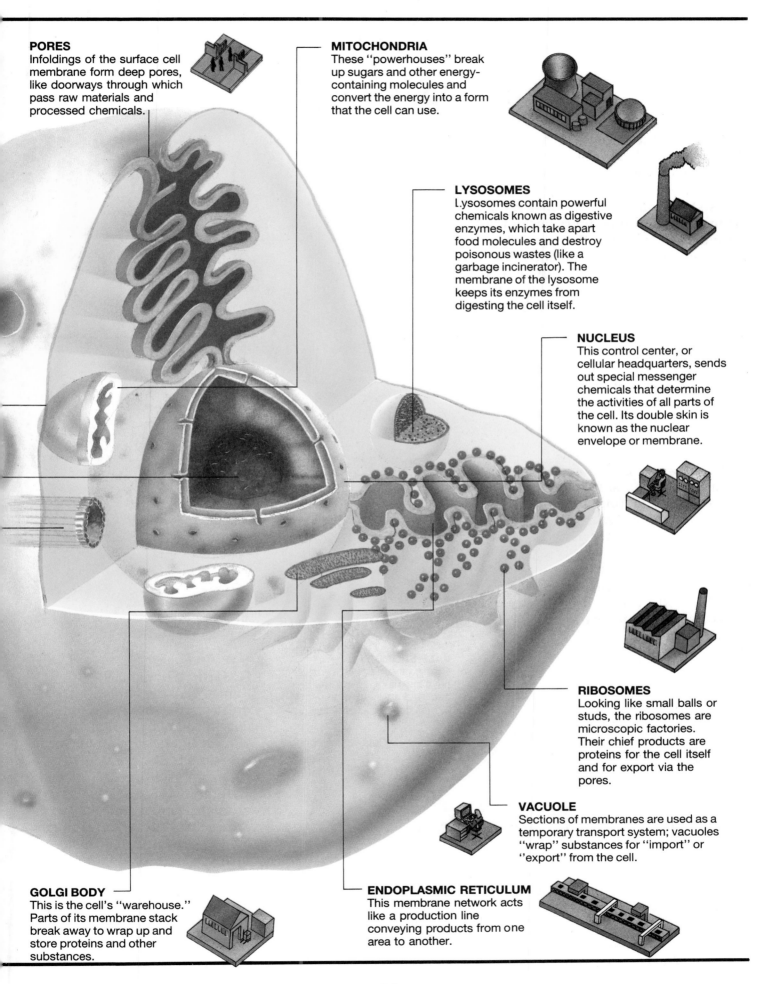

PORES
Infoldings of the surface cell membrane form deep pores, like doorways through which pass raw materials and processed chemicals.

MITOCHONDRIA
These "powerhouses" break up sugars and other energy-containing molecules and convert the energy into a form that the cell can use.

LYSOSOMES
Lysosomes contain powerful chemicals known as digestive enzymes, which take apart food molecules and destroy poisonous wastes (like a garbage incinerator). The membrane of the lysosome keeps its enzymes from digesting the cell itself.

NUCLEUS
This control center, or cellular headquarters, sends out special messenger chemicals that determine the activities of all parts of the cell. Its double skin is known as the nuclear envelope or membrane.

RIBOSOMES
Looking like small balls or studs, the ribosomes are microscopic factories. Their chief products are proteins for the cell itself and for export via the pores.

VACUOLE
Sections of membranes are used as a temporary transport system; vacuoles "wrap" substances for "import" or "export" from the cell.

GOLGI BODY
This is the cell's "warehouse." Parts of its membrane stack break away to wrap up and store proteins and other substances.

ENDOPLASMIC RETICULUM
This membrane network acts like a production line conveying products from one area to another.

MORE CELLS

The world is teeming with countless billions of life forms, each consisting of a single cell. But they are too small for us to see. We are more familiar with bigger living things, whose bodies consist of many cells. In most of these larger animals and plants, there are not only increased numbers of cells, but there are also different kinds of cells in the same body. Each cell's shape, structure, and contents allow it to do a specialized job and contribute to the complex process of keeping the whole body alive.

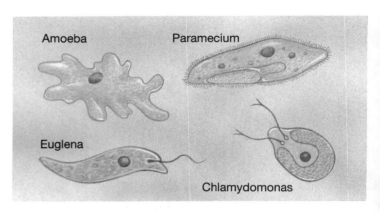

Amoeba

Paramecium

Euglena

Chlamydomonas

SINGLE CELLS

The smallest living things are made of just one cell. They can be seen only under a microscope. Bacteria, one group of single-celled organisms, live in air, soil, water, and in other organisms. They are spherical, rod-shaped, or comma-shaped. Viruses, which are not living cells, are even smaller. Viruses can reproduce only inside other cells. Harmful viruses and bacteria are called germs.

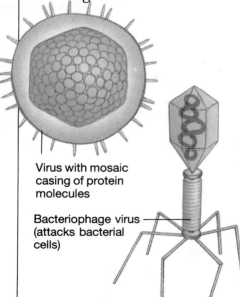

Virus with mosaic casing of protein molecules

Bacteriophage virus (attacks bacterial cells)

SLIME MOLD
This strange sluglike organism is in fact a group of individual cells that exist separately; they come together to produce spores for reproduction.

Slime mold on wood

Single cell

VASE SPONGE
Cells on the inside of the vase have tiny hairs. These hairs beat to draw in water that carries tiny particles of food.

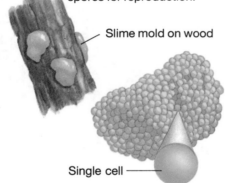

Cutaway of sponge

Water out

Water in

Hairs on inner cells

Volvox colony

Single cell

VOLVOX
Volvox is a colony of cells, rather than a whole organism, that lives in ponds and lakes. Most of the hundred or so cells in the colony are identical.

GROUPS OF CELLS

Some of the smaller, simpler multi-celled organisms are composed of cells that all look similar but cannot all perform the same tasks. They have become specialized. Sponges are among the simplest animals. They cannot move around, see, or feel. But they feed in the typical animal way, by taking in bits of food, breaking these down, and digesting them, instead of building up food from simpler substances, as plants do (page 28).

DIFFERENT ANIMAL CELLS

The body of a big, complex animal is constructed from dozens of different types of cells. A muscle cell is long and thin and specialized so that it can contract, or become shorter. It uses up large amounts of energy so it has lots of mitochondria, the powerhouse organelles. A nerve cell has a very long, thin, wire-like extension, along which nerve signals pass from one part of the body to another. A skin cell is flat, hard, and tough, to protect the delicate body parts beneath. A fat cell is globular and is filled with tiny fat droplets which act as stored energy. A bone cell makes the strong bone structure around it, which is a mixture of proteins and mineral crystals. A blood cell is adapted to carry oxygen.

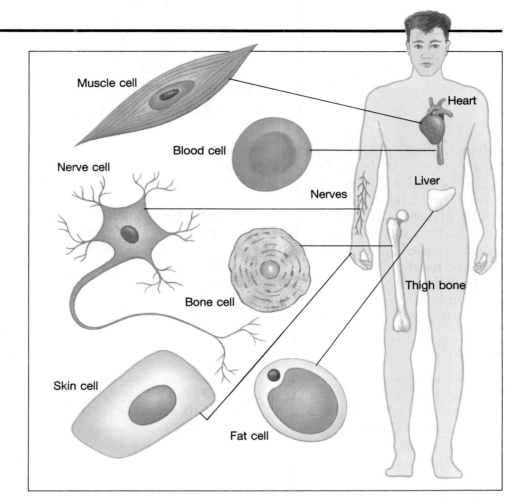

Muscle cell
Heart
Blood cell
Nerve cell
Liver
Nerves
Bone cell
Thigh bone
Skin cell
Fat cell

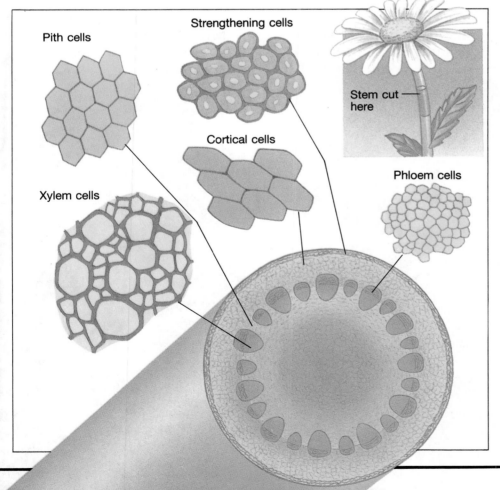

Pith cells
Strengthening cells
Xylem cells
Cortical cells
Stem cut here
Phloem cells

DIFFERENT PLANT CELLS

The cross-section of a flower stem reveals that plants also have many different cells, arranged in groups. Xylem cells are long, hard-walled, tube-shaped, and joined end to end. When they die their contents dissolve away, and the cells then become microscopic tubes through which water flows to reach the different parts of the plant. Phloem cells also form long tubes for conveying food-rich sap around the plant. Pith cells act as "filling" in the stem.

In both animals and plants, layers or groups of similar cells form a structure called a tissue, such as the phloem tissue in a plant, or muscle tissue in an animal. Different combinations of tissues make up the major parts of a plant. In animals these major parts are called organs.

THE TREE OF LIFE

The amazing numbers and varieties of living things may seem bewildering. However, scientists have devised a system of grouping and classifying life forms. This system helps with the study of nature and it shows how life on Earth may have changed through the ages from its microscopic beginnings. The old system of two kingdoms of "plants" and "animals" has been replaced in recent years by a five-kingdom system based partly on differences in cell structure. Even newer systems are being devised.

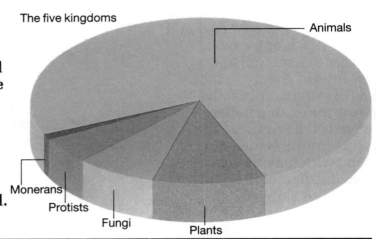

The five kingdoms

Animals
Monerans
Protists
Fungi
Plants

MONERANS

Monerans are the simplest life forms. There are two main groups—bacteria and blue-green algae (cyanobacteria). Their characteristic feature is that their cells do not have a nucleus. Fossils show that monerans were the first life forms on Earth, over 3 billion years ago.

PROTISTS

Protists are mostly single-celled organisms, such as amoebas and tiny algae, or small multi-celled ones in which the cells are all fairly similar. Some feed like animals, by "eating" food. Others are like plants, trapping the energy in sunlight. Some protists can do either.

FUNGI

Fungi are organisms that feed by producing and releasing chemicals that rot down the bodies of other life forms. As the bodies decay and dissolve into simpler substances, the fungi absorb these. Mushrooms, toadstools, yeasts, and slime molds are all fungi.

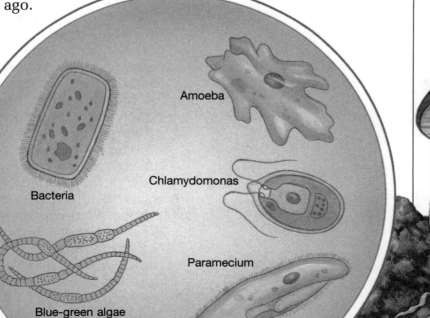

Amoeba

Chlamydomonas

Bacteria

Paramecium

Blue-green algae
(cyanobacteria)

NUMBERS AND SPECIES

Scientists divide living things into basic groups called species. Members of one species look similar to each other, and they can breed with each other to reproduce more of their kind. Members of different species cannot breed successfully. The approximate numbers of species in some major groups are shown here. These are the numbers of species in each group known to scientists at present. Many more may yet be discovered. The insect group has the highest number of species by far.

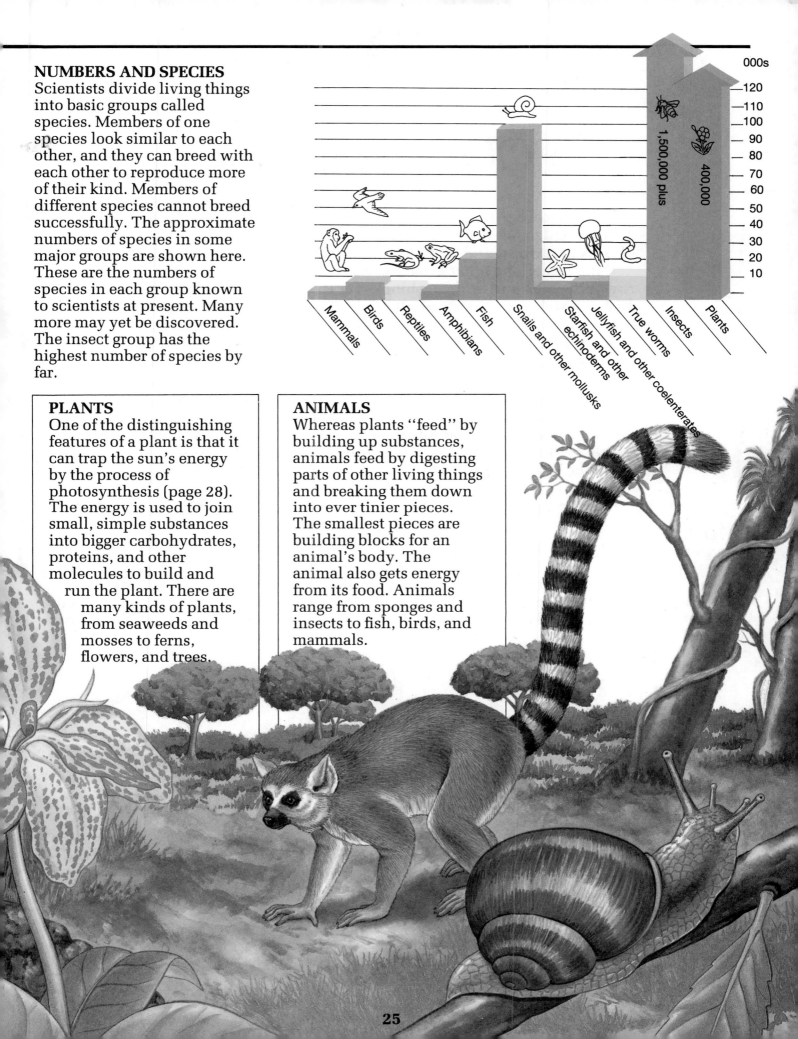

000s
—120
—110
—100
— 90
— 80
— 70
— 60
— 50
— 40
— 30
— 20
— 10

1,500,000 plus

400,000

Mammals · Birds · Reptiles · Amphibians · Fish · Snails and other mollusks · Starfish and other echinoderms · Jellyfish and other coelenterates · True worms · Insects · Plants

PLANTS

One of the distinguishing features of a plant is that it can trap the sun's energy by the process of photosynthesis (page 28). The energy is used to join small, simple substances into bigger carbohydrates, proteins, and other molecules to build and run the plant. There are many kinds of plants, from seaweeds and mosses to ferns, flowers, and trees.

ANIMALS

Whereas plants "feed" by building up substances, animals feed by digesting parts of other living things and breaking them down into ever tinier pieces. The smallest pieces are building blocks for an animal's body. The animal also gets energy from its food. Animals range from sponges and insects to fish, birds, and mammals.

FOOD FOR LIFE

A living body has two major needs. One is energy. The multitude of chemical processes in an organism, and keeping the insides of cells organized and working smoothly, all require energy as a driving force. The other great need is nutrients. These form the raw materials and building blocks for the body's growth, repair, and maintenance. Food, whatever its form, must contain the two basic requirements of energy and nutrients. The feeding links in nature, of who eats what, are an important part of the overall study of how nature works. These feeding links build up to form food chains, which connect together into networks called food webs. Nutrients can be tracked around the food webs, as they are eaten, re-eaten, and recycled by different animals and plants. The source of energy in these food webs can be traced from the meat-eating animals, to the plant-eating animals, to the plants themselves, and ultimately to the sun.

AN OCEAN FOOD WEB

Energy flows from the sun through the plants to the animals. Constructing a food web means knowing the eating habits of each animal. Usually only the main parts of the diet are shown in the web, or the diagram would become impossibly complicated. For example, a polar bear eats a variety of small mammals, birds and their eggs, dying whales, fishes and other creatures, but its main food is seals and sometimes walruses.

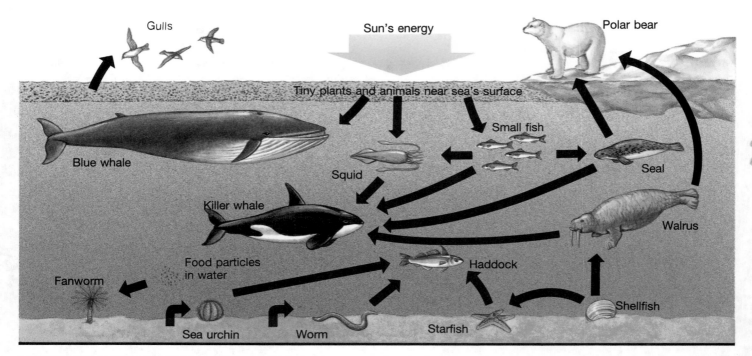

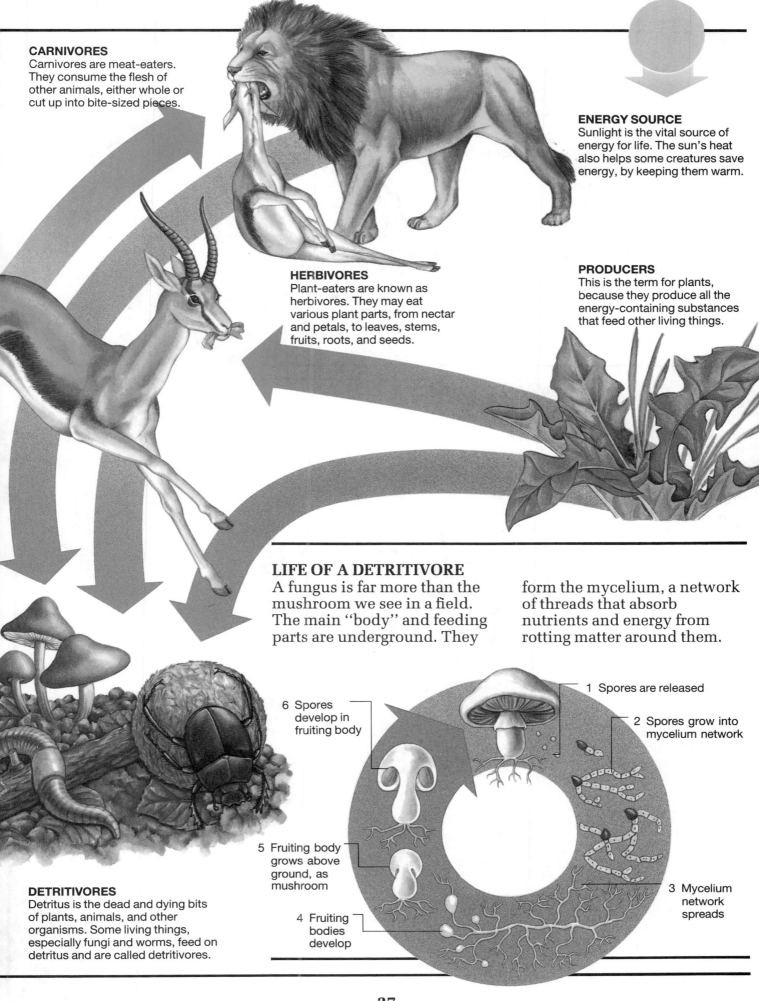

CARNIVORES
Carnivores are meat-eaters. They consume the flesh of other animals, either whole or cut up into bite-sized pieces.

ENERGY SOURCE
Sunlight is the vital source of energy for life. The sun's heat also helps some creatures save energy, by keeping them warm.

HERBIVORES
Plant-eaters are known as herbivores. They may eat various plant parts, from nectar and petals, to leaves, stems, fruits, roots, and seeds.

PRODUCERS
This is the term for plants, because they produce all the energy-containing substances that feed other living things.

LIFE OF A DETRITIVORE
A fungus is far more than the mushroom we see in a field. The main "body" and feeding parts are underground. They form the mycelium, a network of threads that absorb nutrients and energy from rotting matter around them.

1 Spores are released

2 Spores grow into mycelium network

3 Mycelium network spreads

4 Fruiting bodies develop

5 Fruiting body grows above ground, as mushroom

6 Spores develop in fruiting body

DETRITIVORES
Detritus is the dead and dying bits of plants, animals, and other organisms. Some living things, especially fungi and worms, feed on detritus and are called detritivores.

OBTAINING ENERGY

Energy enters the living world through plants. Plants are like natural solar power stations. They capture the energy in the sun's light rays, store it in chemical form, and use it for living and growing. Animals can only survive by "stealing" this energy. They eat plants (or other animals that have eaten plants), thereby taking in the plants' chemical energy supplies. Most of the energy-containing substances are carbohydrates (page 17).

PHOTOSYNTHESIS

Photosynthesis means "making with light." Plants make sugars, which are carbohydrates, by adding energy to form the energy-rich "bonds" between atoms. Plants get the energy to do this from light. They take in small molecules of carbon dioxide and combine them with oxygen and hydrogen from water. They build the small molecules into large molecules, which store the sun's energy.

OCO — Carbon dioxide + HOH — Water → HCHO — Sugar (carbohydrate) + OO — Oxygen

Energy from sunlight

Carbon dioxide in

Oxygen out

Chloroplast

Grana

Granum

Chlorophyll

Membrane systems

Water from roots

Seaweed

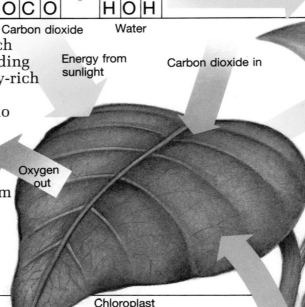

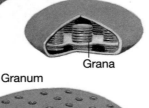

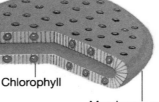

PHOTOSYNTHETIC PIGMENTS

Pigments are the chemicals that trap light energy. The most common pigment is chlorophyll, found in chloroplasts in plant cells. Chlorophyll absorbs red and blue light rays but does not absorb green light. Green light is reflected by the pigments, which is why leaves are green.

ENERGY FROM FOOD

Plants and animals get the energy back out of sugars and other carbohydrates by the process of cellular respiration, which is the "reverse" of photosynthesis. In cellular respiration (page 38), oxygen is needed to break the bonds between the sugar's atoms to release the energy in them.

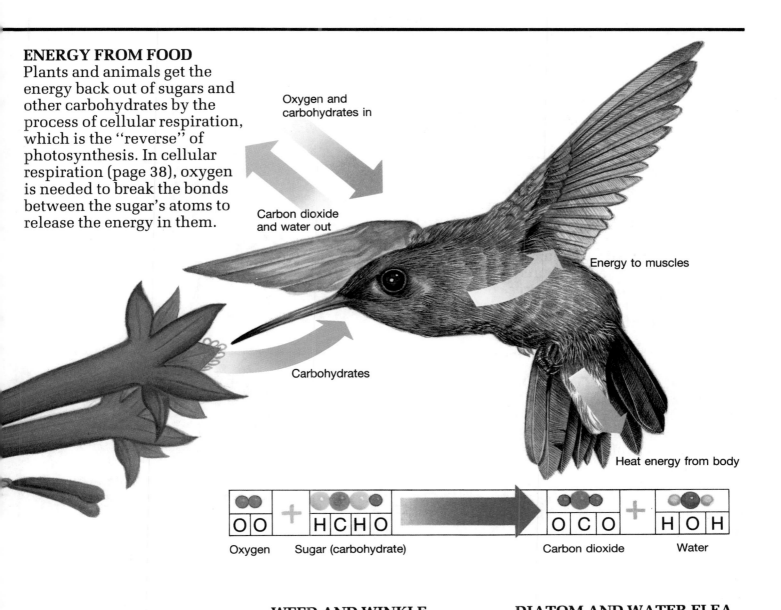

Oxygen and carbohydrates in

Carbon dioxide and water out

Carbohydrates

Energy to muscles

Heat energy from body

Oxygen | Sugar (carbohydrate) | Carbon dioxide | Water

WEED AND WINKLE

It is easy to imagine a fast-flapping hummingbird getting energy from the sweet nectar in a flower. But the basic process is the same in all plants and animals. Seaweeds capture light energy and store it as carbohydrates; periwinkles eat seaweed and use the energy they get from it to fuel their slimy wanderings.

DIATOM AND WATER FLEA

Microscopic plants such as diatoms also trap light energy by photosynthesis and store the energy-rich carbohydrates in their cells. Small creatures such as water fleas graze on the diatoms, taking in the carbohydrates, just as a zebra grazes on grass.

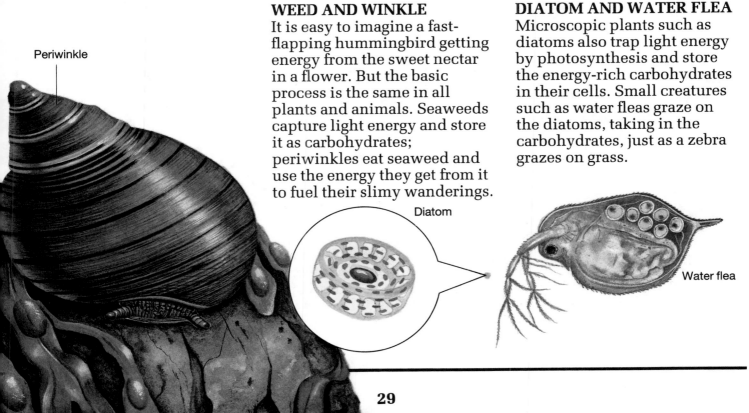

Periwinkle

Diatom

Water flea

ABSORBING FOOD

Plants and animals need a way of protecting the insides of their bodies from the outside world. In tiny water-dwellers the cell membrane does the job. Larger organisms like trees have protective bark, and animals have scales or skin. Somehow the food, containing nutrients and energy, must get through or past this outer protective layer into the organism. Most plants and animals have specialized, thinly-covered areas of the body where nutrients are absorbed, such as roots, mouths, and guts.

ABSORBING DIGESTED FOOD

The tapeworm is a parasite that lives inside the intestine of its host, such as a pig or human. It is surrounded by digested food. The tapeworm simply absorbs the molecules of food through its thin skin into its body sections. Hooks on the tiny head-end stick into the host's intestinal wall, so the tapeworm is not swept away as food moves past.

Roots absorb food from ground

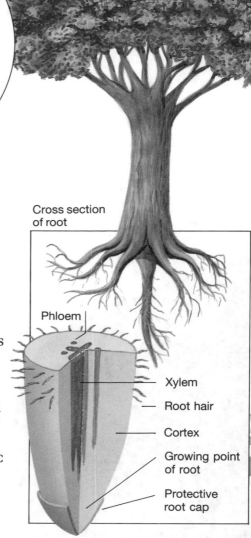

Cross section of root

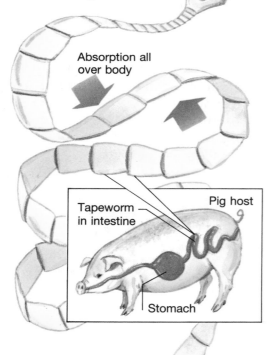

Absorption all over body

Tapeworm in intestine

Pig host

Stomach

ROOT ABSORPTION

Most plants, from daisies to great oak trees, have roots under the ground. The roots anchor the plant in place. They also absorb water, minerals, and other substances from the soil. These nutrients are carried around the plant's body through the network of pipes (xylem and phloem) and are used as building blocks for growth. The main areas for absorption are the microscopic root hairs. Thousands of hairs provide a very large surface area for absorption.

Phloem

Xylem

Root hair

Cortex

Growing point of root

Protective root cap

ALL-OVER ABSORPTION

The microscopic amoeba is a single-celled water-dweller. Its flexible body spreads "arms" around a particle of food. These arms merge and take the food into the amoeba's body. Digestive chemicals from a "bag," called a vacuole, dissolve the food into smaller, easily-used nutrients.

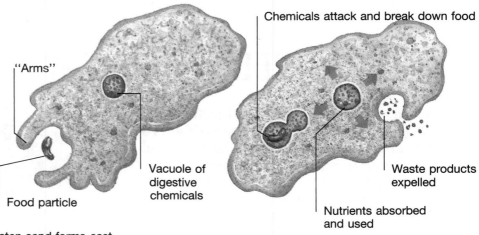

"Arms"

Food particle

Vacuole of digestive chemicals

Chemicals attack and break down food

Waste products expelled

Nutrients absorbed and used

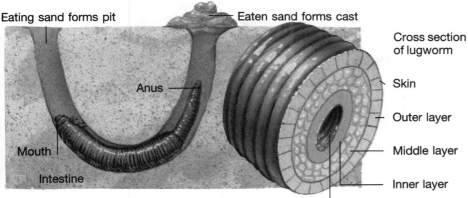

Eating sand forms pit

Eaten sand forms cast

Anus

Mouth

Intestine

Cross section of lugworm

Skin

Outer layer

Middle layer

Inner layer

Food in intestine

ABSORBING FOOD FROM MUD

The lugworm lives under the surface of sandy beaches or muddy estuaries. It eats the sand or mud, which passes through its intestine. Any tiny particles of food are dissolved and absorbed through the intestine wall into its body. Wastes pass out the rear end.

SUCKING UP FOOD

The mosquito has a sharp, tube-shaped mouth like a hypodermic needle. It jabs this tube through the skin of its victim into a small blood vessel below. Then it sucks up its victim's blood, which contains readily-digested nutrients. Its stomach expands like a blood-filled balloon.

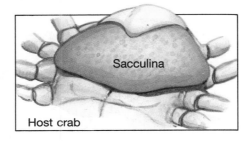

Sacculina

Host crab

FOOD THIEVES

Parasites "steal" food from their hosts. Sacculina is a strange creature with no limbs or head; it is related to the barnacle. It sticks onto the underside of a crab and grows tentacles into the crab's body. These digest and absorb the flesh.

A PLANT FOOD THIEF

Mistletoe is a plant that grows as a part-parasite on other plants, usually trees such as apple, hawthorn, poplar, and linden. It takes in minerals, water, and some food from its host through specialized roots. It also manufactures some of its own food in its leaves by photosynthesis.

Needle mouth (proboscis)

Skin of victim

Hair

Blood vessel

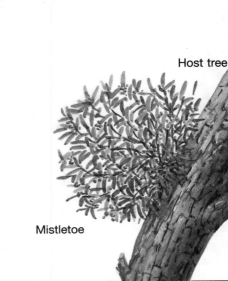

Host tree

Mistletoe

MOUTHS AND EATING

There are as many kinds of mouths, teeth, and jaws in the animal world as there are foods to eat. The crocodile's wide mouth and pointed teeth grab and tear prey such as fish and small antelope. The elephant's teeth are wide and ridged; they grind and chew about 300 pounds of grass and other vegetation each day. Garden snails and slugs rasp and scrape, with their filelike radulas (tongues). Insects possess sharp, pincerlike mouthparts, called mandibles, for dismembering small fish and other little victims.

CAPTURING FOOD
Some animals reach out to grasp their food and pull it to their mouths. The giraffe's long tongue gathers leaves that might otherwise be out of reach. The frog's tongue, octopus's arms, and jellyfish's tentacles all grab and pull in food.

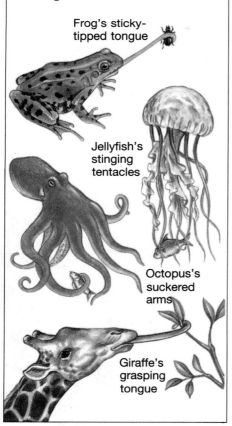

Frog's sticky-tipped tongue

Jellyfish's stinging tentacles

Octopus's suckered arms

Giraffe's grasping tongue

GRINDING AND CHEWING
Strong, wide, ridge-topped teeth are ideal for grinding and mashing. The elephant chews tough grass, and the ray crunches up shellfish.

STABBING AND RIPPING
Sharks, hyenas, and other hunter-scavengers have sharp daggerlike teeth for killing and ripping lumps out of a larger victim.

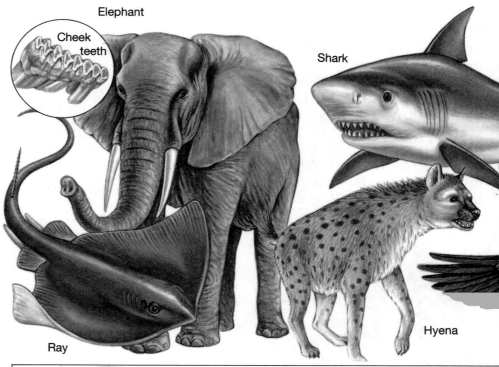

Elephant

Cheek teeth

Shark

Ray

Hyena

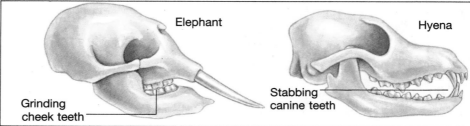

Elephant

Hyena

Grinding cheek teeth

Stabbing canine teeth

SPONGING AND SUCKING

The housefly's mouth is like an absorbent sponge. The fly spits and vomits on its food to dissolve it, then dabs and sucks the resulting liquid.

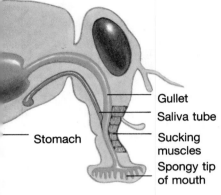

Gullet
Saliva tube
Stomach
Sucking muscles
Spongy tip of mouth

TEARING AND SNIPPING

A powerful, sharp-edged, hooked beak, made of a tough horny substance, allows the octopus and eagle to tear apart their prey.

POISONING

Cobras, vipers, and similar snakes have two long fangs at the front of the mouth. These stab into the victim and inject poison from the poison glands located behind the head.

MORE POISONING

All spiders are killers. They have two sharp, curved fangs for stabbing their prey. Poison (venom) is squirted through a tube in the fang into the prey's body. Each fang hinges against a set of teeth for tearing and crushing.

GULPING AND SWALLOWING

A flexible mouth and gullet is essential for big lumps of food. Pelicans gulp down large fish, and a python can swallow a small deer!

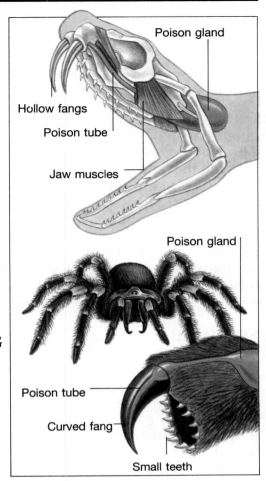

Poison gland
Hollow fangs
Poison tube
Jaw muscles

Poison gland
Poison tube
Curved fang
Small teeth

KILLER PLANTS

Several plants catch and feed on the bodies of small animals. Victims drown in the pitcher plant, get caught between the Venus's-flytrap's leaves, or stick to the sundew.

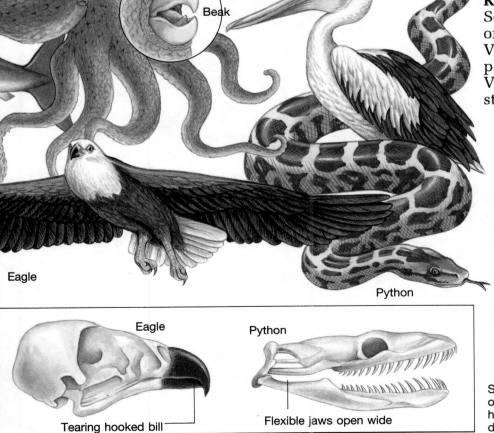

Octopus
Beak
Pelican
Eagle
Python

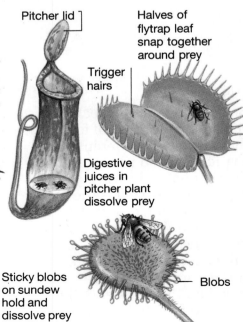

Pitcher lid
Halves of flytrap leaf snap together around prey
Trigger hairs
Digestive juices in pitcher plant dissolve prey
Sticky blobs on sundew hold and dissolve prey
Blobs

Eagle
Tearing hooked bill

Python
Flexible jaws open wide

DIGESTION

Getting food into the digestive system, or gut, is only part of the feeding process. Think of the gut as a long tube running through the animal's body, from mouth to anus. Food in the gut is not truly inside the body. It has not yet passed across the inner "skin" of the gut lining, into the body cells. Digestion involves breaking food into smaller and smaller pieces, until it consists of relatively small molecules. These pass through the gut lining into the body.

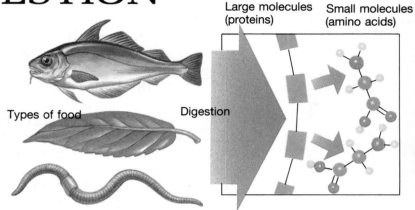

Types of food

Digestion

Large molecules (proteins)   Small molecules (amino acids)

SEA URCHIN

This relative of the starfish has a mouth in the middle of its underside. The mouth leads into a relatively simple gut, which is a long, coiled tube forming the stomach and intestine. The exit is the anus, on the creature's upper side.

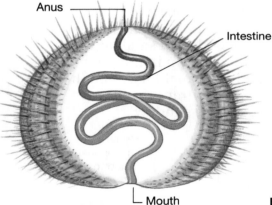

Anus

Intestine

Mouth

INSECTS

Because different insects eat such a huge variety of foods, they have very different guts. Typically, food passes along the esophagus into a storage bag, the crop. Next is the gizzard, which grinds the food, then the mid- and hind-intestines. Dead-end tubes, called caeca, increase the surface area of the gut and speed up the transfer of the digested food to the blood.

MAMMALS

The basic parts of a mammal's gut are: mouth, esophagus (gullet), stomach, small intestine (ileum), large intestine (colon), rectum, and anus. The relative sizes of these vary from one species to another. A meat-eater like a bear has a relatively small gut compared to a plant-eater.

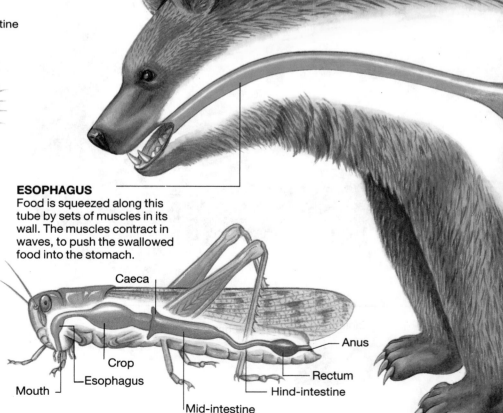

ESOPHAGUS
Food is squeezed along this tube by sets of muscles in its wall. The muscles contract in waves, to push the swallowed food into the stomach.

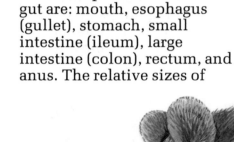

Caeca

Crop

Esophagus

Mouth

Mid-intestine

Anus

Rectum

Hind-intestine

ENZYMES

An enzyme is a molecule that speeds up (or slows down) chemical changes in the body. Digestive enzymes attack and break food into small molecules. Several enzymes occur in the digestive canal, each one attacking a different kind of food. The enzyme amylase occurs in saliva and quickly converts starch to sugar. Pepsin in the stomach begins the breakdown of proteins.

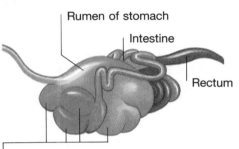

Rumen of stomach

Intestine

Rectum

Other chambers of stomach

RUMINANTS

Cows, sheep, deer, camels, and similar types of mammals are ruminants. Their large stomachs have several chambers. Chewed food is partly digested in the first chamber, the rumen. The animal then brings it up and chews it again, known as "chewing the cud," before it passes to the other chambers of the stomach and beyond.

BIRDS

Like an insect, the typical bird has a crop and gizzard. The expandable crop means the bird can eat lots of food in a short time and then fly away to avoid predators. The gizzard grinds up tough foods such as seeds, often with the help of grit which the bird swallows.

STOMACH
Food is stored in this large bag. It is squashed into a soup by the stomach's squirming movements and attacked by strong digestive chemicals.

LARGE INTESTINE
Water and minerals pass from the soupy undigested food here back into the body for recycling. The digestive leftovers form semi-solid wastes, the feces.

SMALL INTESTINE
More digestive chemicals continue the breakdown process in this area. It is also the main absorbing section, as nutrients pass through the intestine's thin lining into the blood vessels beyond.

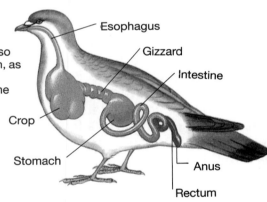

Esophagus

Gizzard

Intestine

Crop

Stomach

Anus

Rectum

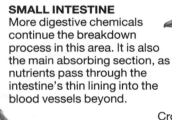

RECTUM
The feces are stored in this expandable section of the gut, until the animal is ready to expel them through the last part, the anus.

HELPFUL BACTERIA
Plant-eaters like the proboscis monkey have bacteria in their guts that digest the walls of plant cells and release the nutrients.

GETTING RID OF WASTES

A living organism takes in building-block nutrients and high-energy foods and uses them in many different body processes. As a result, by-products of body chemistry, undigested bits of food, and other types of wastes have to be removed. In most animals there are two separate and distinct kinds of wastes: the leftovers from digestion, and waste products made in the cells. These two kinds of wastes are collected and expelled in very different ways. The removal of wastes made in the body is called excretion.

Oxygen

Food
Drink

Carbon dioxide
Water

Urine

Feces

THE DEBRIS OF LIVING

It is fairly easy to dispose of undigested and leftover food from the gut. The remains pass out of the body, usually through a closeable ring of muscle, the anus. But throughout the body, in every living cell, waste molecules are produced as a result of life's chemical processes. Some are useless; others are harmful if they accumulate. In creatures made of one or a few cells, the wastes can easily pass to the outside through the cell membranes. More complicated bodies require a system for collecting this waste, called urine, and expelling it.

Wastes absorbed

Wastes disposed
with leftover food
through anus

Hindgut

Malpighian tubule

Midgut

INSECTS
In insects, the blood collects wastes from around the body. Long, thin malpighian tubules float in the blood and absorb wastes, passing them into the gut for disposal.

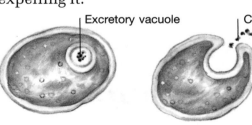

Excretory vacuole

Contents expelled

AMOEBA
In this simple one-celled protist, wastes collect in an excretory vacuole. This joins with the cell wall and empties its contents into the surrounding water.

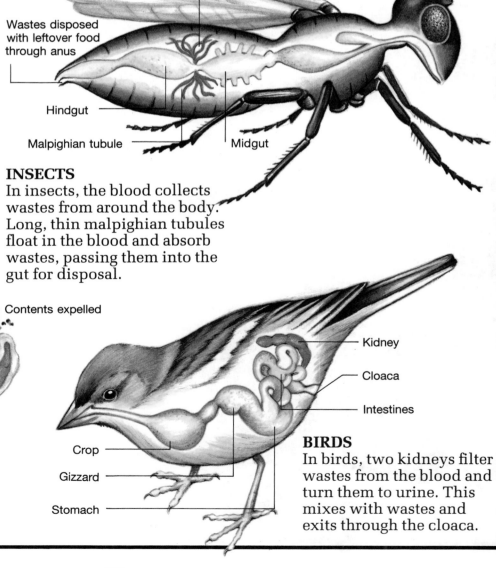

Kidney

Cloaca

Intestines

Crop

Gizzard

Stomach

BIRDS
In birds, two kidneys filter wastes from the blood and turn them to urine. This mixes with wastes and exits through the cloaca.

THE PROBLEMS OF SALT

Fresh water has fewer chemicals in it than body fluids do. Water enters a freshwater creature, making its body fluids more dilute. So creatures such as fish must continually get rid of this excess water by making lots of dilute urine. In sea water the problem is reversed. A salmon must change its waste disposal methods as it moves from sea to river.

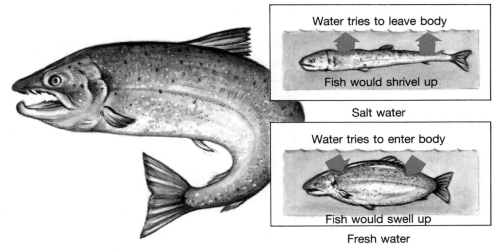

Water tries to leave body
Fish would shrivel up
Salt water

Water tries to enter body
Fish would swell up
Fresh water

MAMMALS

Waste disposal is carried out by the excretory system. In a mammal like an orangutan this consists of kidneys that filter blood to make waste urine, ureters that take the urine to the bladder for storage, and a urethra to expel the urine. Each kidney has a million microscopic nephrons, or filtering units. Waste passes from the blood in the glomerulus into the nephron's tubule. Urine trickles out the other end of the tubule, into the main kidney space.

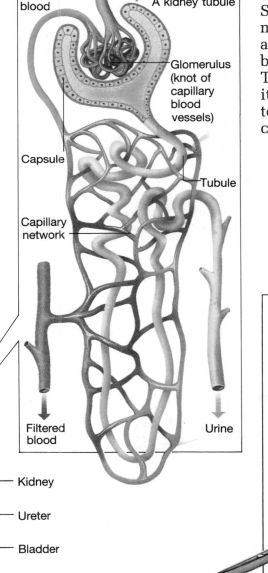

Unfiltered blood

A kidney tubule

Glomerulus (knot of capillary blood vessels)

Capsule

Tubule

Capillary network

Filtered blood

Urine

Orangutan

Kidney

Ureter

Bladder

Urethra

EXCRETION IN PLANTS

Sometimes a plant takes up more water than it requires. and more than it can get rid of by evaporation from its leaves. The excess water oozes from its leaves as droplets and drips to the ground. This process is called guttation.

TOO MUCH SALT

Sea birds such as gulls, albatrosses, and pelicans eat salty fish. The extra salt causes problems with the body chemistry so it is expelled as very salty "tears" from glands near their eyes and trickles down their beaks.

Salt gland

Salty "tears"

RESPIRATION AND CIRCULATION

Apart from a few bacteria and other small organisms, living things can survive only if they have oxygen. Oxygen plays a vital role in the chemical reactions during which energy-containing molecules in food are "burned" to release their energy. Oxygen cannot be stored in a plant or animal, so it must be taken in continuously from the surroundings.

There are two phases to the process of respiration. One is gas-exchange respiration. The organism takes in oxygen, and in exchange it gives out the waste product carbon dioxide. The parts of the animals and plants shown here that are involved in gas exchange are colored blue. Once in the body, the oxygen is spread around by a circulatory system. The second phase is cellular respiration, the series of chemical reactions in each cell that makes energy available for processes of living.

FLATWORM
No part of this creature's leaf-shaped body is far from its thin skin. Oxygen dissolved in the water around it can easily spread through its body.

All-over absorption through thin skin

Gills on back

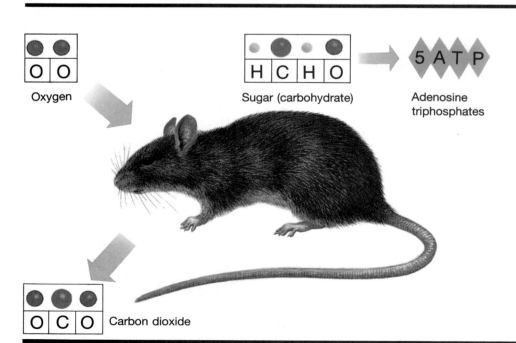

Oxygen

Sugar (carbohydrate)

5 A T P

Adenosine triphosphates

Carbon dioxide

CELLULAR RESPIRATION
Oxygen is used to break apart a variety of energy-containing molecules, such as sugars (carbohydrates) and fats. The molecules pass through a series of more than a dozen chemical reactions. End results include waste carbon dioxide and numerous molecules of the energy-rich substance ATP (adenosine triphosphate). ATP molecules are then shunted around the cell and used to drive its many other chemical processes. This type of respiration is also known as aerobic respiration.

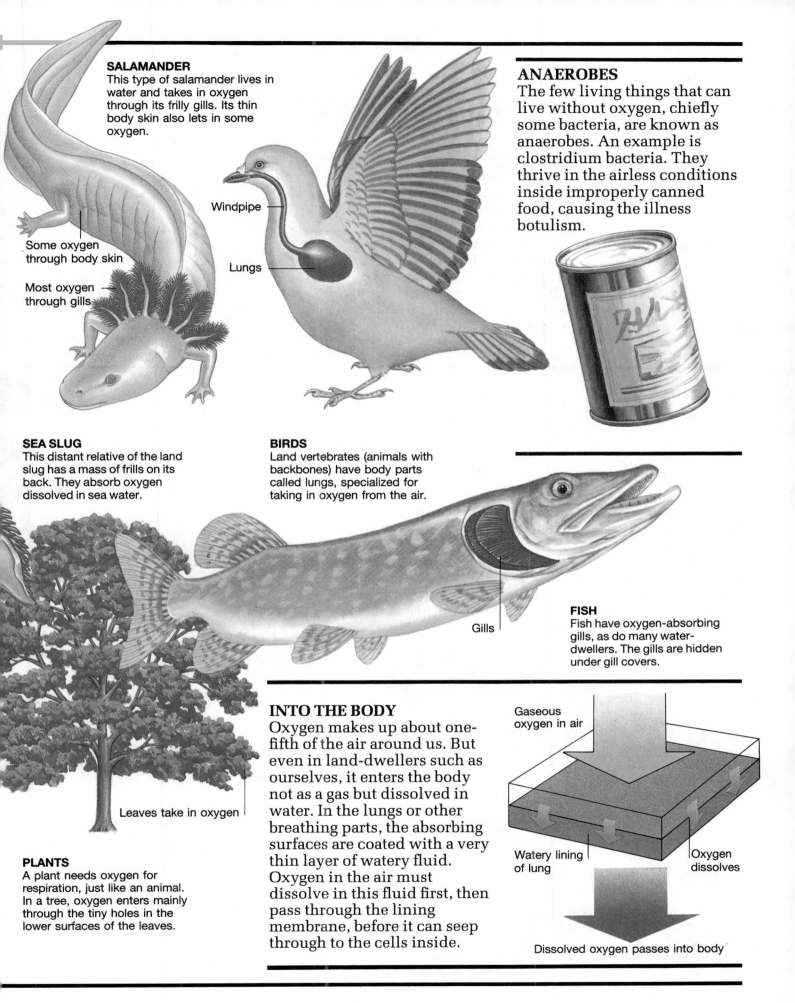

SALAMANDER
This type of salamander lives in water and takes in oxygen through its frilly gills. Its thin body skin also lets in some oxygen.

Some oxygen through body skin

Most oxygen through gills

Windpipe

Lungs

ANAEROBES
The few living things that can live without oxygen, chiefly some bacteria, are known as anaerobes. An example is clostridium bacteria. They thrive in the airless conditions inside improperly canned food, causing the illness botulism.

SEA SLUG
This distant relative of the land slug has a mass of frills on its back. They absorb oxygen dissolved in sea water.

BIRDS
Land vertebrates (animals with backbones) have body parts called lungs, specialized for taking in oxygen from the air.

Gills

FISH
Fish have oxygen-absorbing gills, as do many water-dwellers. The gills are hidden under gill covers.

Leaves take in oxygen

PLANTS
A plant needs oxygen for respiration, just like an animal. In a tree, oxygen enters mainly through the tiny holes in the lower surfaces of the leaves.

INTO THE BODY
Oxygen makes up about one-fifth of the air around us. But even in land-dwellers such as ourselves, it enters the body not as a gas but dissolved in water. In the lungs or other breathing parts, the absorbing surfaces are coated with a very thin layer of watery fluid. Oxygen in the air must dissolve in this fluid first, then pass through the lining membrane, before it can seep through to the cells inside.

Gaseous oxygen in air

Watery lining of lung

Oxygen dissolves

Dissolved oxygen passes into body

GETTING OXYGEN

The key to taking in plentiful oxygen is a large surface covered by a thin skin. The bigger the surface area, the more oxygen can pass through it. And thin skin is less of a barrier to the passage of oxygen. In animals there are two basic designs for oxygen-obtaining parts. One is an outgrowth—a tree-like structure with leafy branches. The other is an ingrowth—a hole or pit, with folds and lobes. It is important to keep air or water moving past these parts in order to bring fresh supplies of oxygen.

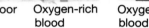

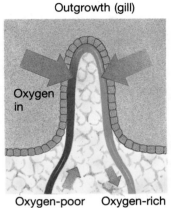

Outgrowth (gill)

Oxygen in

Oxygen-poor blood   Oxygen-rich blood

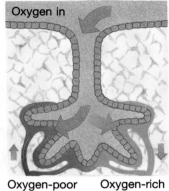

Ingrowth (lung)

Oxygen in

Oxygen-poor blood   Oxygen-rich blood

INSECTS

Land animals have the "ingrowth" design. In insects this takes the form of tiny holes, called spiracles, along the body. The holes lead into a network of tubes, known as tracheae, which branch and become smaller. Their ends are called tracheoles, which touch inner parts such as muscles and the gut. Oxygen passes from the outside air, along the tubes, and is absorbed by the inner parts.

FISH

Aquatic (water-dwelling) creatures use the "outgrowth" design for absorbing oxygen. The oxygen-obtaining parts are called gills. Their many feathery filaments give a huge surface area for taking in dissolved oxygen from the water. The oxygen passes easily through the very thin, delicate "skin" of the gill filaments, into the blood flowing just beneath.

Water out past gills

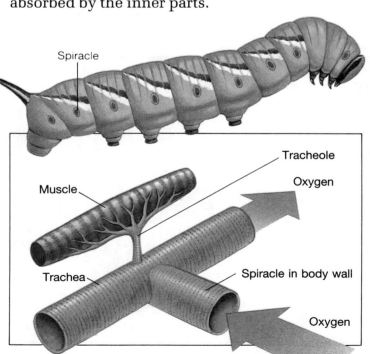

Spiracle

Tracheole

Oxygen

Muscle

Trachea

Spiracle in body wall

Oxygen

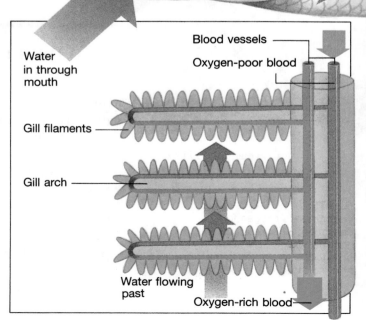

Water in through mouth

Blood vessels

Oxygen-poor blood

Gill filaments

Gill arch

Water flowing past

Oxygen-rich blood

SPIDER

Some spiders have "book" lungs. The "pages" of the book form a large surface area. Muscle movements pump the air in and out through an opening in the body casing.

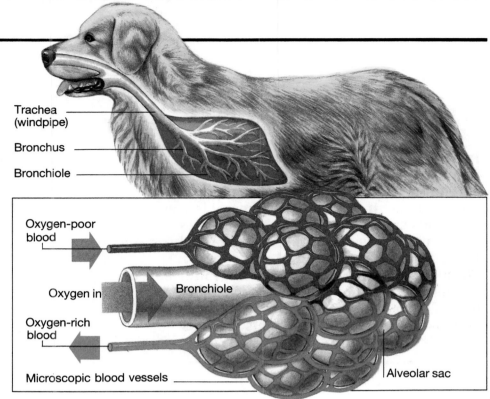

Trachea (windpipe)

Bronchus

Bronchiole

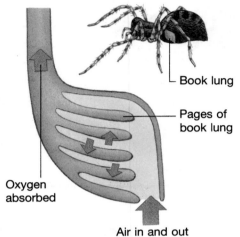

Book lung

Pages of book lung

Oxygen absorbed

Air in and out

Oxygen-poor blood

Oxygen in

Bronchiole

Oxygen-rich blood

Microscopic blood vessels

Alveolar sac

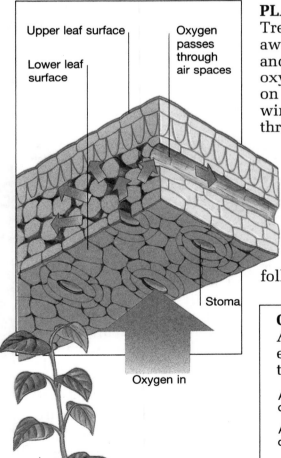

Upper leaf surface

Lower leaf surface

Oxygen passes through air spaces

Stoma

Oxygen in

PLANTS

Trees cannot breathe to blow away stale oxygen-poor air and replace it with fresh oxygen-rich air. They depend on natural air movements—wind. Oxygen passes in through stomata, or holes, which are mainly on the undersides of the leaves. It spreads through the honeycomb of air spaces in the leaf, then dissolves in the fluid covering the cells to reach their interiors. Carbon dioxide follows the reverse path.

MAMMALS

Mammalian lungs have a huge surface area, due to millions of microscopic air sacs known as alveoli. Oxygen reaches them along a branching system of air tubes, the bronchi and bronchioles. It passes through the alveolar wall and is carried away by blood flowing through vessels on the other side. Fresh air is sucked into the lungs, and stale air is blown out, by the movements of breathing produced by the chest and abdomen muscles.

OXYGEN NEEDS

Active animals use more energy than inactive ones, so they need more oxygen. Cold-blooded creatures need less oxygen than warm-blooded ones of the same size.

A slug has low oxygen needs

A snake has medium oxygen needs

A squirrel has high oxygen needs

A bird has very high oxygen needs

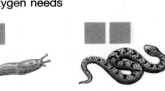

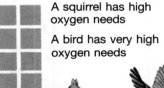

CIRCULATION

In a tiny animal such as a flatworm, oxygen can reach all parts of the body by diffusion—spreading from places where it is plentiful and highly concentrated to areas where it is scarce. Nutrients spread around the body in the same way. But in other creatures, and especially on land, diffusion is too slow. A transport or circulatory system is needed to carry nutrients or oxygen, or both, around the body in a fluid called blood. Even a tiny mosquito has its own blood, which carries digested nutrients, from its victim's blood, around its own body.

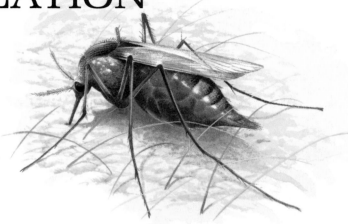

SNAIL

Most animals have blood, a special fluid that circulates, or flows around, the body. It may travel in tubes all the way, or for only part of its journey. In many invertebrates (creatures without backbones), blood leaves blood vessels and seeps among body organs and through spaces called sinuses. In the snail it flows around the single lung and picks up oxygen, then goes to the heart and is pumped into vessels that distribute it to the body parts and sinuses again.

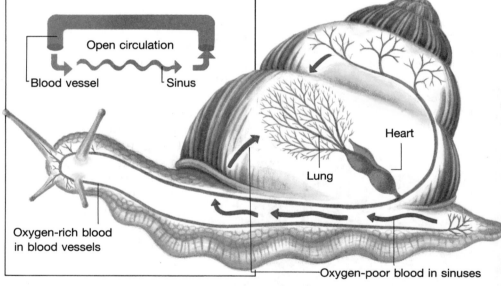

Open circulation

Blood vessel — Sinus

Oxygen-rich blood in blood vessels

Heart

Lung

Oxygen-poor blood in sinuses

Closed circulation

Lungs

Heart

Body

Oxygen-poor blood

Oxygen-rich blood

Cerebral artery to brain

Main arteries

Main veins

Heart

MAMMALS

Unlike the open circulation of a snail, mammals such as elephants have a closed circulatory system, where blood remains mostly in its tubes. The heart is a double-sided pump (page 44), and the circulatory system has two parts. One side of the heart sends blood to the lungs to pick up oxygen; this is known as the pulmonary circulation. The blood returns to the heart's other side and is then pumped all around the body; this is the systemic circulation.

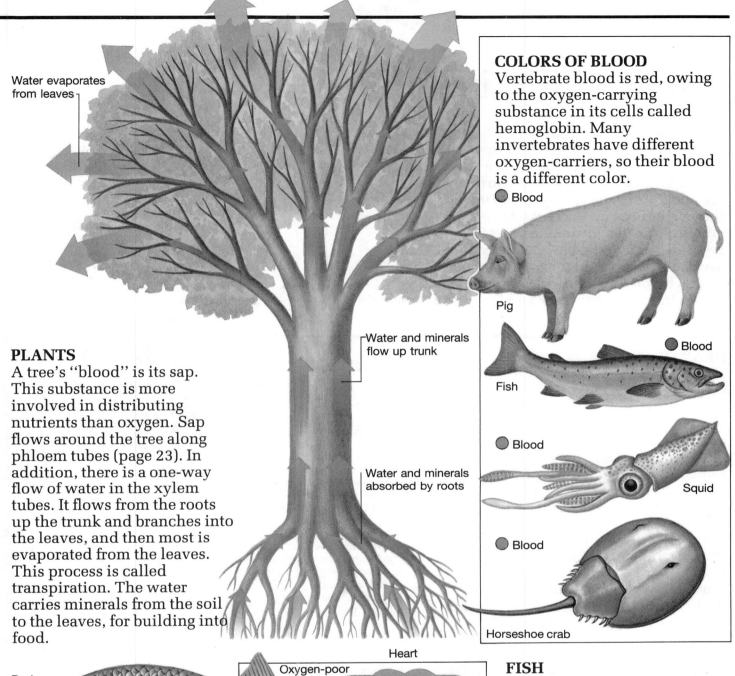

Water evaporates from leaves

Water and minerals flow up trunk

Water and minerals absorbed by roots

PLANTS

A tree's "blood" is its sap. This substance is more involved in distributing nutrients than oxygen. Sap flows around the tree along phloem tubes (page 23). In addition, there is a one-way flow of water in the xylem tubes. It flows from the roots up the trunk and branches into the leaves, and then most is evaporated from the leaves. This process is called transpiration. The water carries minerals from the soil to the leaves, for building into food.

COLORS OF BLOOD

Vertebrate blood is red, owing to the oxygen-carrying substance in its cells called hemoglobin. Many invertebrates have different oxygen-carriers, so their blood is a different color.

● Blood

Pig

● Blood

Fish

● Blood

Squid

● Blood

Horseshoe crab

FISH

In contrast to the double-pump heart and the two-part circulation of a mammal (described opposite), the fish heart is a single pump. It receives low-oxygen blood from all over the body, and sends this to the gills to receive fresh supplies of oxygen. The blood continues to flow along vessels that carry it all around the body, distributing the oxygen and also nutrients. The body parts use the oxygen, and the blood flows slowly back to the heart.

Body

Heart

Gills

Heart

Oxygen-poor blood

Horseshoe

Ventricle

Atrium

Body

Gills

Oxygen-rich blood

HEART AND BLOOD

Very small, simple animals can do without a heart. The squeezing effects of their muscles, as they move, breathe, and feed, are sufficient to massage the blood vessels and propel blood around the circulatory system. However, from tiny water fleas up to great whales, most creatures need a muscular heart to pump regularly and make the blood circulate. There are usually valves in the heart and main vessels, so that blood flows steadily in one direction, rather than sloshing back and forth going nowhere.

Water flea's heart

HEARTS

Mammals have the most complex heart (right). It has two pumps, each with two chambers and a one-way valve. The left pump sends blood around the body; the right one sends it to the lungs (page 42). The bird heart is similar. Many reptile and amphibian hearts have three chambers. One receives blood from the lungs, the second from the body, and the third sends blood to lungs and body. An insect heart consists of about five bulges along the main blood vessel.

Pulmonary artery

Pulmonary valve

Tricuspid valve

MAIN VEINS
The venae cavae are two large veins that bring blood, collected by smaller veins all around the body, back to the right atrium.

RIGHT ATRIUM
This thin-walled upper chamber swells with blood in each heartbeat, and passes its contents through the valve to the right ventricle below.

RIGHT VENTRICLE
The ventricles are large, thick-walled pumping chambers. The right one sends oxygen-poor blood along the pulmonary artery to the lungs.

Tendon supporting valve

1 Blood flows from the main veins into the upper chambers, the atria

2 The blood passes through valves to the lower ventricles

Muscle of heart wall

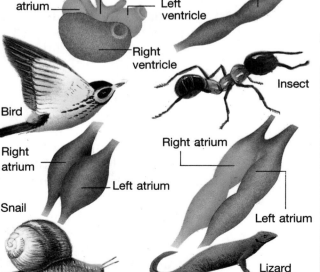

Muscle bulge of heart

Left atrium

Right atrium

Left ventricle

Right ventricle

Bird

Insect

Right atrium

Right atrium

Left atrium

Left atrium

Snail

Lizard

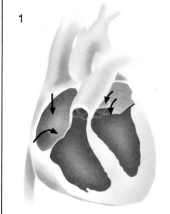

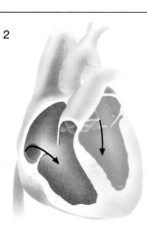

1

2

3

Blood from heart

Artery

Lumen (blood space)

AORTA
This is the body's biggest blood vessel. It contains oxygen-rich blood pumped forcefully from the left ventricle. It branches to distribute the blood around the body.

Endothelium (lining)

Outer sheath

PULMONARY VEIN
The pulmonary veins convey oxygen-rich blood from the lungs to the left atrium. From here it squirts through the valve into the left ventricle.

Thick muscle and elastic layer

Capillary

Lumen

Left atrium

Single-celled wall

Septum

Oxygen and nutrients

Aortic valve

Carbon dioxide and wastes

Bicuspid (mitral) valve

Left ventricle

Tissues

Right ventricle

3 The ventricles squeeze blood out through more valves into the main arteries

4 The atria refill with blood, and the whole cycle starts again

Vein

4

Valve

Thin muscle and elastic layer

Outer sheath

Endothelium (lining)

To heart

Lumen (blood space)

BLOOD VESSELS
There are three main kinds of blood vessels: arteries, capillaries, and veins. Arteries take blood away from the heart. They generally carry oxygen-rich blood (except pulmonary arteries, which transport oxygen-poor blood from heart to lungs). They have strong, muscular walls, to withstand the pressurized surges of blood with each heartbeat. Arteries divide many times to form capillaries, microscopic vessels with very thin walls. Oxygen and nutrients pass from the blood, through the capillary walls, to the cells beyond. The capillaries join together to make large, thin-walled, floppy veins, the third type of vessel. These channel the blood back to the heart. In a human body, two-thirds of the blood is flowing through the veins at any time.

HEART RATES
On average, the human heart beats about 70 times a minute. Other animals have different rates. In general, the hearts of small animals beat faster than those of larger ones.

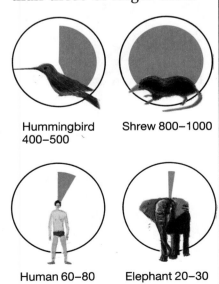

Hummingbird 400–500

Shrew 800–1000

Human 60–80

Elephant 20–30

GROWING AND MOVING

Growth is one of the major features of life. Most animals and plants begin small and grow into larger adults so that they can survive better and reproduce. Simple organisms grow by adding more of the same cells, as in a volvox colony. (The basic method of making more cells, mitosis, is described on page 74.) More complex organisms get bigger by increasing the numbers of cells in the body and making these cells different from each other, in the process called development. Growth can occur in all parts of the body, so that the adult looks like an enlarged version of the young plant or animal. Or growth may happen at specialized growing points, so that the organism changes its appearance as it gets larger. Movement may be part of growth, but usually it is a separate ability, confined to animals, protists, monerans, and very few fungi.

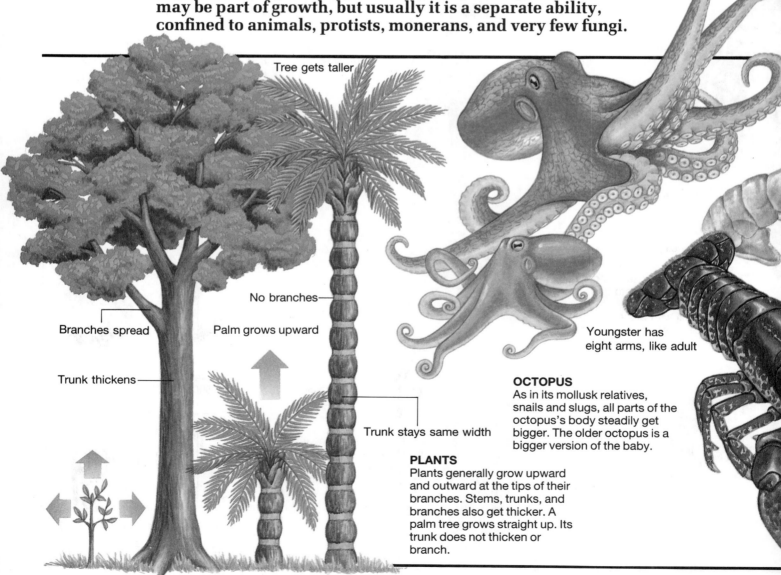

Tree gets taller

Branches spread

Palm grows upward

No branches

Trunk thickens

Trunk stays same width

Youngster has eight arms, like adult

OCTOPUS
As in its mollusk relatives, snails and slugs, all parts of the octopus's body steadily get bigger. The older octopus is a bigger version of the baby.

PLANTS
Plants generally grow upward and outward at the tips of their branches. Stems, trunks, and branches also get thicker. A palm tree grows straight up. Its trunk does not thicken or branch.

GROWTH AND CHANGE

In certain animal groups, members change their appearance markedly as they grow. This change of form is called metamorphosis. It is most familiar to us in insects, as shown here. Partial change is known as incomplete metamorphosis; drastic change is complete metamorphosis. Amphibians also go through metamorphosis. A frog lays eggs. Eggs hatch into tadpoles, which develop and change into adult frogs.

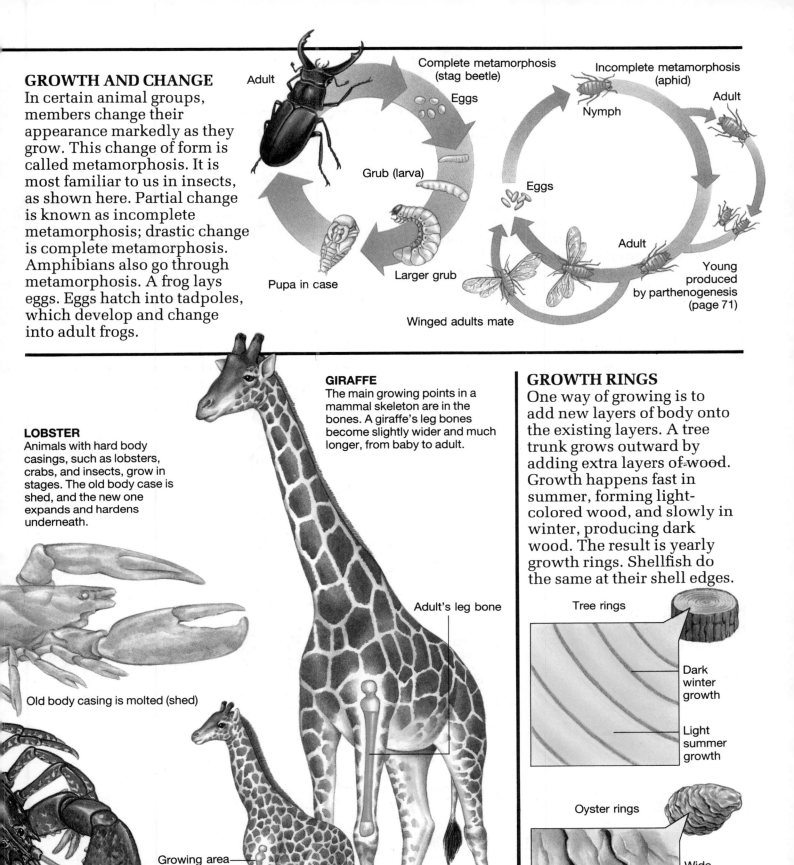

Adult

Complete metamorphosis (stag beetle)

Eggs

Grub (larva)

Larger grub

Pupa in case

Winged adults mate

Incomplete metamorphosis (aphid)

Nymph

Adult

Eggs

Adult

Young produced by parthenogenesis (page 71)

LOBSTER
Animals with hard body casings, such as lobsters, crabs, and insects, grow in stages. The old body case is shed, and the new one expands and hardens underneath.

Old body casing is molted (shed)

GIRAFFE
The main growing points in a mammal skeleton are in the bones. A giraffe's leg bones become slightly wider and much longer, from baby to adult.

Adult's leg bone

Growing area

Baby's leg bone

GROWTH RINGS
One way of growing is to add new layers of body onto the existing layers. A tree trunk grows outward by adding extra layers of wood. Growth happens fast in summer, forming light-colored wood, and slowly in winter, producing dark wood. The result is yearly growth rings. Shellfish do the same at their shell edges.

Tree rings

Dark winter growth

Light summer growth

Oyster rings

Wide summer growth

Growth stops in winter

MOVEMENTS 1

Nearly all animals make movements within their own bodies, as they feed, digest, circulate blood, and expel wastes. But not all animals move about. Barnacles and oysters stay stuck on seashore rocks. Corals and sponges remain in the same place in shallow water throughout their lives. If conditions become unfavorable, or if food runs out, they die. Animals that can move about have great advantages. They are able to search for food, avoid being eaten, and escape bad conditions in search of better ones.

WALKING

Limbs (arms and legs) enable an animal to hold its main body clear of the ground and move it along in a series of swinging steps. Usually, animals that have long, slim limbs are able to walk and run faster than those with short, thick limbs. The typical limb bends at several points along its length, known as joints. After making a step, the limb bends up, forward, and back to the ground, ready to make the next step.

RUNNING
Many running animals "bounce" along, touching the ground briefly as they push themselves forward and up, then arching through the air.

CROCODILE
The crocodile bends its limbs back and forth, and also arches its long body from side to side as it walks along.

Body bends to right

Legs move forward   Legs move back

Body bends to left

Legs move back   Legs move forward

SPIDER
Eight limbs need careful control, or a spider may trip itself! The limbs move forward, one after the other.

Back legs in   Back legs out

CRAB
A crab's limbs bend sideways under its body, instead of forward and back. This is why crabs run sideways.

Front legs out   Front legs in

Cheetah

Back legs push off   Mid-air   Front legs land   Back arches   Back legs land

Horse

Back legs push off   Takeoff   Mid-air   Front legs land   Front legs stride

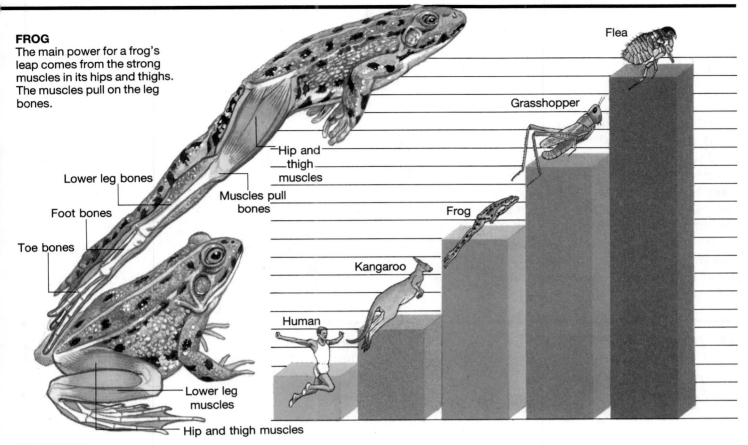

FROG
The main power for a frog's leap comes from the strong muscles in its hips and thighs. The muscles pull on the leg bones.

Lower leg bones

Foot bones

Toe bones

Hip and thigh muscles

Muscles pull bones

Lower leg muscles

Hip and thigh muscles

Flea

Grasshopper

Frog

Kangaroo

Human

LEAPING
Leaping is a series of jumps, between which the creature may come to a standstill. Strong muscles, usually in the back legs, are needed to accelerate the whole body from a sitting start. The leg joints straighten like a series of levers, from the hip to the knee and ankle. The graph shows that small creatures leap farther, relative to their body size, than big ones.

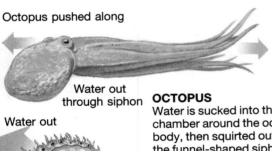

Octopus pushed along

Water out through siphon

Water out

Water in

OCTOPUS
Water is sucked into the large chamber around the octopus's body, then squirted out through the funnel-shaped siphon. This makes the octopus move backward.

Water in

SCALLOP
This mollusk draws water into its body chamber by slowly opening its shell. As the shell snaps shut, water shoots out and jerks the scallop backward.

SQUIRTING
Various aquatic animals move using the jet propulsion principle. They slowly take water into a body cavity, then contract the muscles in the cavity walls. This contraction squeezes the water so that it jets powerfully out of a small hole and shoots the animal along.

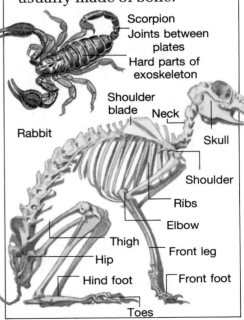

SKELETONS
Invertebrates such as scorpions and insects have a hard outer body case called an exoskeleton. Vertebrates such as mammals have an internal or endoskeleton, usually made of bone.

Scorpion

Joints between plates

Hard parts of exoskeleton

Shoulder blade

Neck

Skull

Rabbit

Shoulder

Ribs

Elbow

Thigh

Hip

Front leg

Hind foot

Front foot

Toes

MOVEMENTS 2

Land animals push against the ground as they walk and run, or slide over it as they slither. Air and water are not firm solids like the ground. They are fluids, and if you push against them they tend to flow out of the way. So long, slim limbs are not very effective for swimming and flying. Broad, wide surfaces give a stronger push against air or water. This is the basic design for the wings of fliers such as birds and bats, and the fins and tails of swimmers such as fish and whales.

FLYING

A wing's downstroke forces air down and back, causing the creature to be pushed up and forward. The upstroke is less powerful because the wing is tilted or altered in some way, so the air is able to slip past and does not push the animal down again.

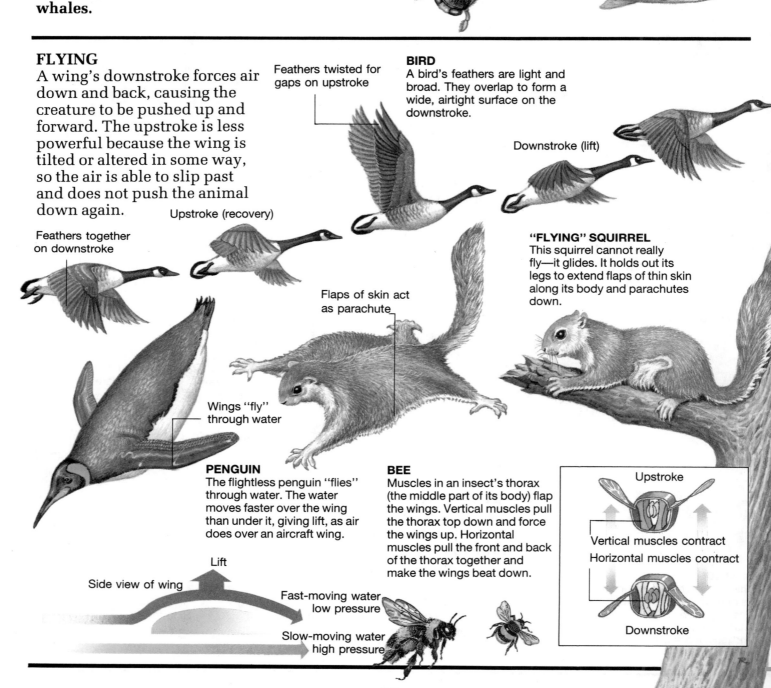

Feathers twisted for gaps on upstroke

Upstroke (recovery)

Feathers together on downstroke

BIRD
A bird's feathers are light and broad. They overlap to form a wide, airtight surface on the downstroke.

Downstroke (lift)

"FLYING" SQUIRREL
This squirrel cannot really fly—it glides. It holds out its legs to extend flaps of thin skin along its body and parachutes down.

Flaps of skin act as parachute

Wings "fly" through water

PENGUIN
The flightless penguin "flies" through water. The water moves faster over the wing than under it, giving lift, as air does over an aircraft wing.

BEE
Muscles in an insect's thorax (the middle part of its body) flap the wings. Vertical muscles pull the thorax top down and force the wings up. Horizontal muscles pull the front and back of the thorax together and make the wings beat down.

Lift

Side view of wing

Fast-moving water low pressure

Slow-moving water high pressure

Upstroke

Vertical muscles contract

Horizontal muscles contract

Downstroke

ROWING

The movements of rowing in water are similar to those of flying in air. A flat, broad surface such as a fin pushes the water back, and the water, in turn, pushes the animal's body forward. Many different body structures are used as "oars" in this way.

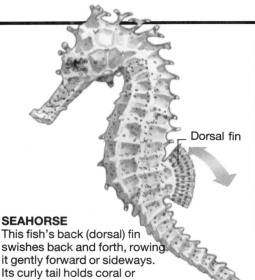

Paramecium moves along

Cilia

Power stroke   Recovery stroke

Close-up of cilia

PARAMECIUM
This protist, a microscopic pond-dweller, has many tiny hairs, called cilia, over its body. They row with a wave-like motion.

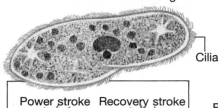

Water flea moves along

Recovery stroke

Power stroke

Antennae

WATER FLEA
This pinhead-sized pond crustacean rows with its outsized, branching antennae, sprouting from its head!

SWIMMING

Some fish swim slowly by rowing with their fins, but for most of the larger aquatic animals the main swimming organ is the tail. It swishes back and forth, pushing water backward, and propelling the owner forward as a result.

WHALE
A whale arches its body up and down to make the swishing movements of the tail, called the flukes.

Dorsal fin

SEAHORSE
This fish's back (dorsal) fin swishes back and forth, rowing it gently forward or sideways. Its curly tail holds coral or weed.

Bristles fold together

Bristles spread wide

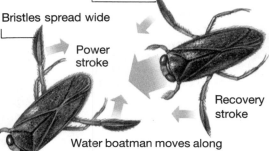

Power stroke

Recovery stroke

Water boatman moves along

WATER BOATMAN
Bristles on this insect's back rowing legs spread on the power stroke, to give a broader surface for pushing the water.

Lobster moves along

Tail bends rapidly

LOBSTER
When in danger, the lobster straightens its tail and then folds it with a snap under its body to jerk itself backward.

JOINTS
Animals with stiff, rigid skeletons find it very difficult to move. Most skeletons have flexible joints between their parts, especially in the limbs. At the joint of an exoskeleton, the outer body case is very thin and bendy.

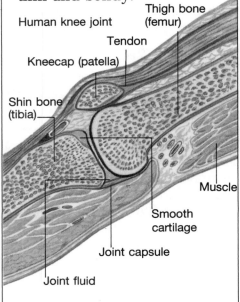

Human knee joint

Thigh bone (femur)

Tendon

Kneecap (patella)

Shin bone (tibia)

Muscle

Smooth cartilage

Joint capsule

Joint fluid

Insect "knee"

Thin casing at joint

Upper part of limb

Lower part of limb

Muscle

Insect body

Exoskeleton of limb

Exoskeleton around body

Muscles inside exoskeleton

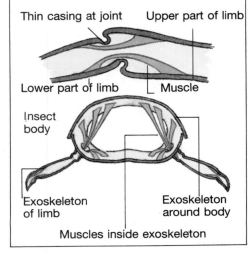

Body arches from side to side

FISH
A fish bends its body from side to side, to make the tail swish. The tail is also known as the caudal fin.

Fish swims along

Body arches up

Body arches down

MOVEMENTS 3

Not all animals have to chase after their food or race away from danger. Some creatures take their lives at a slower pace. Instead of walking and running, they use other methods of moving that do not require limbs. These methods have their own advantages. The humble earthworm is able to wriggle and burrow through soil. A snail can grip and glide over the slipperiest of surfaces. And the snake, though legless, is not only a speedy slitherer; it can also swim well, burrow in soft soil, and even climb trees!

SLITHERING

The slithers of snakes and worms are controlled by batches of muscles along the body. Each batch bends a section of the body. By contracting the muscles in part of one side of the body, then the other, an S-shaped bend moves along the body.

EARTHWORM

In its burrow, the worm moves by elongation (opposite). On the soil's surface, it wriggles from side to side, more like a snake.

Worm in burrow

Body arches like a snake

Body segments

Tiny hairs grip ground

Snake moves forward

Bend 1 here

Bend 1 moved to here

Bend 2 starting here

Bend 2 now here

Bend 3 starting here

Bend 1 now here

Muscles tensed

Muscles relaxing

Skink swims by arching body

SKINK
The desert skink, a type of lizard, can hardly walk on its tiny legs. It "swims" through loose sand, like an eel in water.

SNAIL
Waves of muscle contraction ripple along the snail's foot, propelling it forward, but only at 33 feet per hour (we walk 400 times faster!).

Muscular ripples   Trail of mucus

SNAKE
Serpentine S-bends flow along the body of the snake. It grips the ground with the tilted edges of its belly scales, and so propels itself forward.

SLIDING
Snails and slugs ooze a trail of thick slime from the "foot," the lower part of the body. The slime, or mucus, helps them to grip smooth surfaces such as glossy leaves.

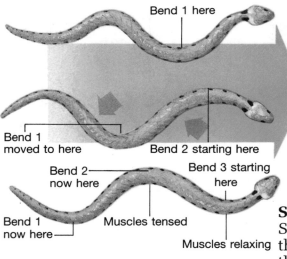

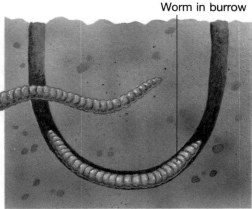

Snail slides along

MUSCLES

In all but the simplest creatures, moving power is provided by muscles. Inside a muscle are long, thin fibers, and inside the fibers are long, thin fibrils. A fibril contains bundles of two types of molecules, actin and myosin. These slide past each other, like toothed bars, and interlock to make the muscle shorter or longer. The shortening, or contraction, uses lots of energy. Muscles can only pull; they cannot push. So for two-way movements at a joint, they are arranged in opposing pairs. One muscle pulls and moves the joint, stretching its relaxed partner. The partner pulls the joint back.

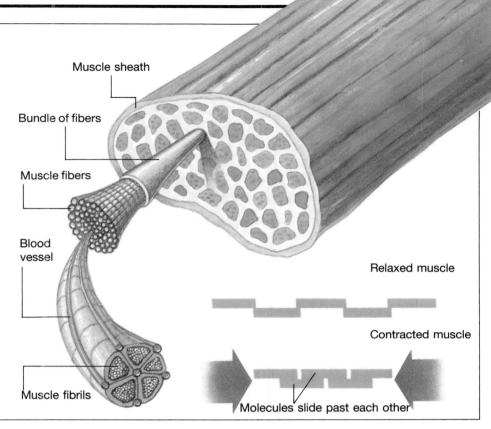

Muscle sheath

Bundle of fibers

Muscle fibers

Blood vessel

Muscle fibrils

Relaxed muscle

Contracted muscle

Molecules slide past each other

OTHER MOVEMENTS

Burrowing and tunneling creatures have to push and squash the soil aside, so they need specially modified body parts and strong muscles. Such animals tend to make slow but steady movements rather than fast, jerking ones.

SLIME MOLD
For part of their life, bits of slime mold fungus come together to form a crawling, sluglike organism.

2 Slime-mould colony crawls

1 Separate parts of slime mold collect

AMOEBA
This protist oozes along by sticking out "arms" called pseudopodia; the rest of the body then flows into them.

Arm extends

Head pushes forward

Front of body is thicker

Middle of body is thicker

SPADEFOOT TOAD
Small lumps on the rear feet of this toad (really a frog) help it to burrow backward into the soil if danger is near.

"Spade"

MOLE
The mole has short but wide and powerful front legs, with long claws. It uses these like spades, to dig away the soil and push it to the side.

Head and snout push forward

Rear of body is thicker

EARTHWORM
The worm extends its front end, makes this end thicker to press on the tunnel wall, and then draws up its rear.

Claws

Shell anchored in sand

Foot forces into sand and swells

Shell drawn down

RAZOR CLAM
This fast-burrowing clam pushes its foot into the sand and pulls its shell behind.

Foot contracts

Front feet dig earth and push it backward

THE SENSES

The ability to move is a great advantage for most animals. But where should they move to, and when, and why? Most do not stumble about blindly, unaware of their surroundings. Even the simplest worms and tiny pond creatures have some senses. Senses make an animal aware of its environment. We are familiar with our own five senses: sight, hearing, smell, taste, and touch. Each sense organ detects a feature of the surroundings, makes a pattern of nerve signals, and sends these to the brain (page 65). Our lives are dominated by sight and hearing. Other creatures rely on different senses, depending on where and how they live. Also, our senses have limits. Dogs, bats, and dolphins hear ultrasounds, which are too high-pitched for our own ears. Many animals have senses that we lack. Some are sensitive to the Earth's natural magnetic field, or to the tiny bursts of electricity sent out by living organisms.

THE SENSITIVE SHARK

A superb hunter, the shark is equipped with a wide range of senses that tell it what is happening in its watery world.

TASTE AND SMELL

For animals that live in air, these senses are usually separate. In water, both senses detect waterborne chemicals, and both are referred to as chemoreception (page 60).

SIGHT

The shark sees near objects quite clearly, but its vision is limited over longer distances. This is not usually a drawback, since the water may be cloudy anyway.

ELECTRICITY

Small pits around the head, the ampullae of Lorenzini, lead to sense organs that respond to minute electrical signals sent out by the active muscles of nearby animals.

MAGNETISM

It is not clear if sharks detect the invisible lines of force from the Earth's weak magnetic field. We still have much to learn about animal senses.

PROPRIOCEPTION

Animals have microscopic sensors called proprioceptors in their bodies. These tell them about the position of their muscles, skeleton, and other body parts as they move.

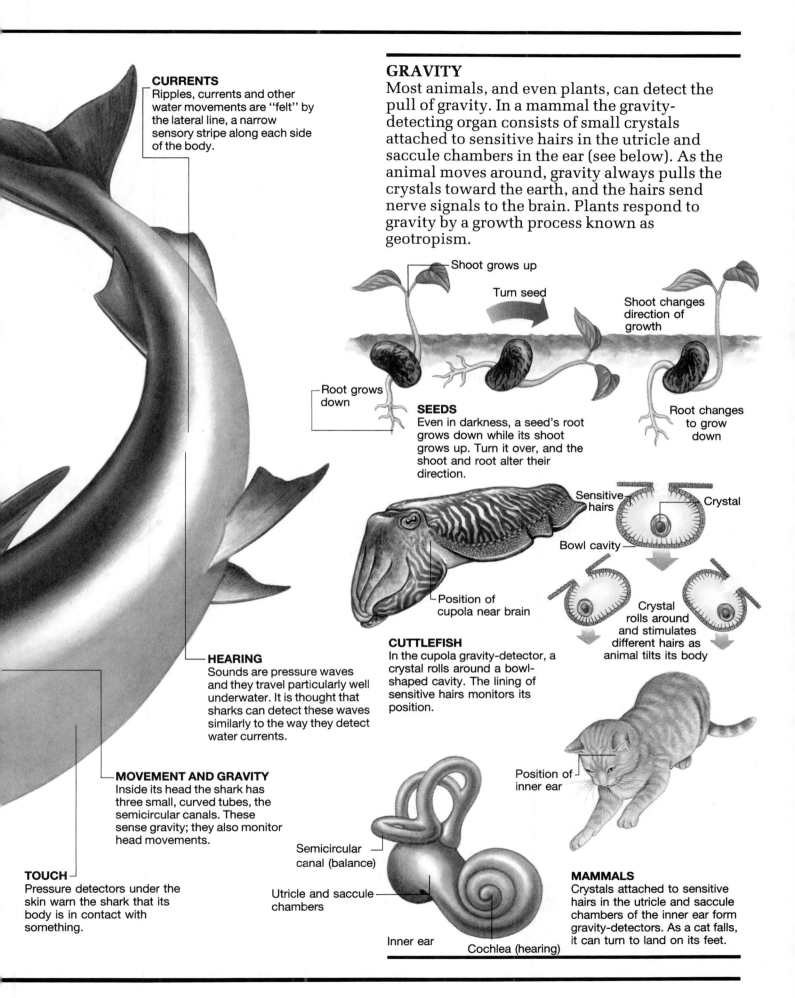

CURRENTS
Ripples, currents and other water movements are "felt" by the lateral line, a narrow sensory stripe along each side of the body.

GRAVITY

Most animals, and even plants, can detect the pull of gravity. In a mammal the gravity-detecting organ consists of small crystals attached to sensitive hairs in the utricle and saccule chambers in the ear (see below). As the animal moves around, gravity always pulls the crystals toward the earth, and the hairs send nerve signals to the brain. Plants respond to gravity by a growth process known as geotropism.

Shoot grows up

Turn seed

Shoot changes direction of growth

Root grows down

Root changes to grow down

SEEDS
Even in darkness, a seed's root grows down while its shoot grows up. Turn it over, and the shoot and root alter their direction.

Sensitive hairs

Crystal

Bowl cavity

Crystal rolls around and stimulates different hairs as animal tilts its body

Position of cupola near brain

CUTTLEFISH
In the cupola gravity-detector, a crystal rolls around a bowl-shaped cavity. The lining of sensitive hairs monitors its position.

HEARING
Sounds are pressure waves and they travel particularly well underwater. It is thought that sharks can detect these waves similarly to the way they detect water currents.

MOVEMENT AND GRAVITY
Inside its head the shark has three small, curved tubes, the semicircular canals. These sense gravity; they also monitor head movements.

Position of inner ear

TOUCH
Pressure detectors under the skin warn the shark that its body is in contact with something.

Semicircular canal (balance)

Utricle and saccule chambers

Inner ear

Cochlea (hearing)

MAMMALS
Crystals attached to sensitive hairs in the utricle and saccule chambers of the inner ear form gravity-detectors. As a cat falls, it can turn to land on its feet.

LIGHT, MAGNETISM, ELECTRICITY

Light rays are very useful. They inform an animal about objects, colors, and movements that are still a long way away. If these mean danger, the animal has plenty of time to make its escape. This is why most animals, other than those that live mainly underground or in deep sea, have some sense of sight. A magnetic sense helps some creatures on their long migrations around the world, and the ability to detect electrical impulses helps creatures underwater (electrical signals do not travel well through air).

SIGHT

Each major group of animals has evolved its own design for the organ that detects light—the eye. In a bird or mammal eye, light rays come in through the transparent cornea. They are focused by the lens to give a clear, unblurred image on the layer at the back of the eye, the retina. Millions of light-sensitive cells in the retina convert the energy of light rays into minute electrical pulses, or nerve signals, which pass along the optic nerve to the brain.

INSIDE A VULTURE'S EYE
This bird has extremely good sight. The central part of its field of vision is magnified to pick out small objects, like its prey!

Magnified central image

Background image

Focusing muscle

Iris

Cornea

Lens

Pecten

Choroid and sclera

Optic nerve

Retina

Clear jelly

THE "DAY'S EYE"
The daisy's name originated as "day's eye." The flower opens its petals in the morning, as though opening its eye, and closes them at dusk.

Daisy open in day   Daisy closed at night

PLANTS
Many plants detect the direction of the sun's rays. Their leaves and flowers swivel throughout the day, to get maximum light for growth.

Sunflower faces morning sun

Sunflower turns to follow sun

MAGNETISM

A small magnet strapped to a homing pigeon may confuse the bird's ability to find its way home. It seems that various animals have a "natural compass." They are sensitive to our planet's north-south magnetic field. Their magnetic sense helps them to make long migrations over land or through featureless oceans. Despite much scientific research, the organs that detect magnetism, and how they work, are still unclear.

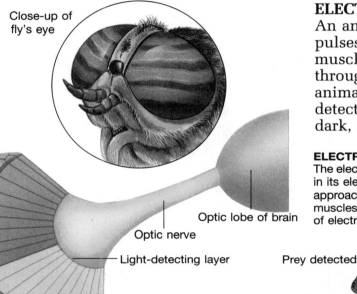

North Pole

Invisible lines of magnetic force

Birds

Insects

Whales

South Pole

INSIDE AN INSECT'S EYE

A horse-fly's eye has hundreds of separate light-detecting units, called ommatidia. Each one picks up light from a small part of the scene. So the insect may receive a patchy, mosaic-type view of the world.

Close-up of fly's eye

Optic lobe of brain

Optic nerve

Light-detecting layer

Ommatidium

Lens

Insect eye's view?

ELECTRICITY

An animal produces weak pulses of electricity in its muscles. These travel well through water. Some aquatic animals can use the pulses to detect and stun prey, even in dark, muddy water.

ELECTRIC EEL

The electric eel senses changes in its electric field when prey approaches. Its specialized muscles then give out a big jolt of electricity to stun the victim.

Prey detected

Prey shocked

POLARIZED LIGHT

Even when it is cloudy, a bee knows where the Sun is. It sees the direction of filtering, or polarization, of the sunlight.

Light polarized by atmosphere and clouds

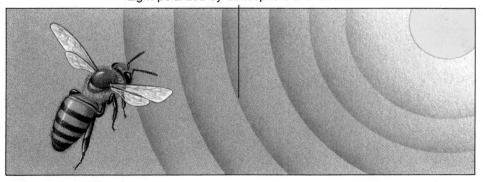

ELEPHANT-SNOUT FISH

This fish makes weak electrical signals, which are altered by nearby prey animals.

Ray

Elephant-snout fish

Worm

Shellfish

RAY

A ray senses the electrical pulses given out by its shellfish meal, even when this is buried in the sand.

SOUND AND VIBRATIONS

Sound waves are sets of vibrations, in the form of tiny back and forth movements of molecules, spreading outward from their source. The vibrations pass through a substance, such as air, water, or a solid material. Ears and other vibration-detecting parts pick up the movements of the molecules and convert them to nerve signals, which are sent to the brain. Like sight, hearing is an at-a-distance sense. It can give advance warning of danger, or food, or the approach of a mating partner or family member.

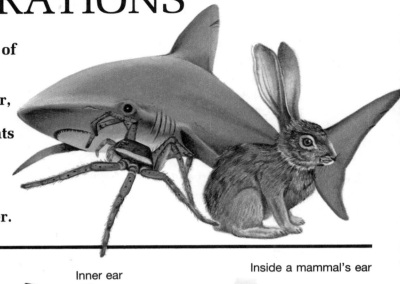

VIBRATIONS IN AIR

Most hearing organs have a thin, flexible membrane called the eardrum. Sound waves make this membrane vibrate. The eardrum's vibrations are passed inward and are detected by tiny hairs in the cochlea that generate nerve signals.

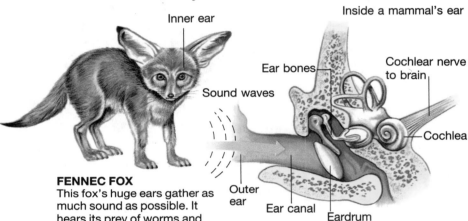

Inside a mammal's ear

Inner ear

Ear bones

Cochlear nerve to brain

Sound waves

Cochlea

Outer ear

Ear canal

Eardrum

FENNEC FOX
This fox's huge ears gather as much sound as possible. It hears its prey of worms and insects moving about in the desert sand.

CRICKET
Sounds are important to this insect—males chirp to attract females, who listen carefully. The "ears" are on the abdomen or front legs!

Ears on legs or abdomen

FROG
In many frogs, the eardrum is a disk of thin skin just behind the eye. Frogs listen to their own croaks and those of mates.

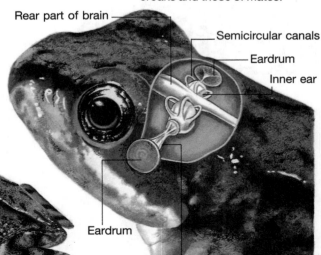

Rear part of brain

Semicircular canals

Eardrum

Inner ear

Eardrum

Ear bones

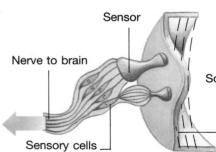

Sensor

Nerve to brain

Sound waves

Sensory cells

Eardrum (tympanic membrane)

VIBRATIONS IN WATER

Sounds travel four times faster in water than in air. There are other water movements too, such as currents, surface waves, and the ripples of passing animals. The main vibration-detecting organ of a fish is its lateral line.

FISH

A fish's lateral line consists of a groove or tube that runs along each side of the body and contains sensitive hairs. Water movements rock the hairs and generate nerve signals.

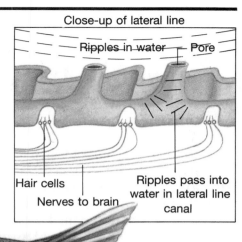

Close-up of lateral line

Ripples in water — Pore

Hair cells

Nerves to brain

Ripples pass into water in lateral line canal

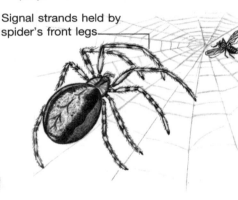

Lateral line of a dace

VIBRATIONS IN SOLIDS

Sound waves and other forms of vibrations travel many times faster through solids than through air or water. However they usually fade away in a shorter distance. Predators can detect the movements of their prey if their sense of touch is tuned in to the vibrations.

SPIDER

A spider holds on to special strands at the edge of its web. When these shake or vibrate, the spider runs out to grab its prey.

Signal strands held by spider's front legs

DEATHWATCH BEETLE

An eerie "tap-tap" sound coming from old oak beams may be a deathwatch beetle, knocking on the wood with its jaws. This is its mating call!

Beetle taps with jaws

BIRDS

Watch a blackbird on a lawn. It pauses and cocks its head, listening for sounds of worms coming through the soil and then the air.

Vibrations from worm's movements pass through soil

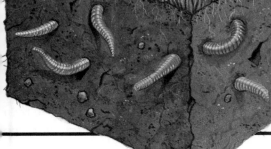

PITCH

A sound's frequency is its pitch (low or high). Different animals hear different frequency ranges.

Pitch

High

Mouse

Great whale

Human

Low

Elephant

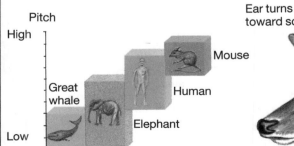

DIRECTION

Deer, horses, rabbits, and other animals swivel their ears without turning the head, to locate the direction of a sound.

Ear turns toward sound

Ears move separately

TASTE AND SMELL

Our own noses are not particularly sensitive to smells. So we cannot really appreciate how much information a creature such as a wolf receives from its surroundings simply by sniffing the air. Animals use smell signals to mark their territories and, in the case of the skunk, as an effective defense! The sense of taste is important to all kinds of animals.

NOSES AND TONGUES

A smell is molecules of a chemical wafting through the air, detected in the nose. A taste is molecules of a chemical in a liquid or solid, sensed by the tongue. Both these sense organs check that food is suitable to eat.

MAMMALS
Molecules dissolve in the watery lining in the nose and stimulate the hair cells of the olfactory organ.

Nerve signals to brain

Brain

Olfactory bulb

Nasal cavity

Smell sniffed in

Mouth

Tongue

Taste buds on tongue

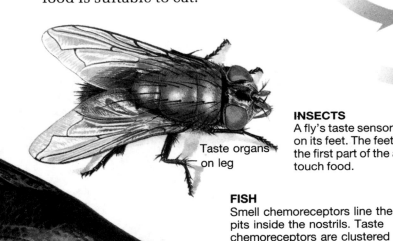

Taste organs on leg

INSECTS
A fly's taste sensors are located on its feet. The feet are usually the first part of the animal to touch food.

FISH
Smell chemoreceptors line the pits inside the nostrils. Taste chemoreceptors are clustered on the head and in the mouth.

Nostril

Taste receptors in mouth lining

CHEMORECEPTION
For water creatures, all chemicals are carried in the water. So smell and taste are similar and are both known as chemoreception. A shark can detect only one part of blood in a million parts of water!

PHEROMONES
A pheromone is a scent signal, made and released by an animal to affect another animal (usually of the same species). The smeller detects it and is stimulated to carry out some action or behavior. Bees in a hive respond to alarm pheromones released by their members who are attacked; they swarm around and sting the attacker.

MOTH
A female moth attracts males by producing a pheromone that the males smell with their feathery antennae.

Nerve signals to brain

Close-up of antenna

Male moth

Antenna

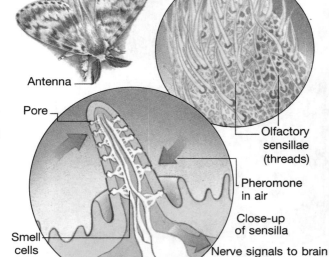

Pore

Olfactory sensillae (threads)

Pheromone in air

Close-up of sensilla

Smell cells

Nerve signals to brain

TOUCH AND TIME

The most immediate sense is touch, or feeling. It signals to an animal or a plant that it is in physical contact with something. The most mysterious sense is time. Numerous creatures seem to have a "body clock" that records the passing of time and regulates their behavior. Animals can also sense by an internal thermometer when their bodies are hot or cold.

Dermis (inner layer)

Epidermis (outer layer)

Hair

Hair follicle

TOUCH AND SKIN

Mammal skin is especially sensitive to touch, unlike the hard body casings of creatures such as insects. Touch is a complex sense, and the skin possesses numerous types of microscopic sensors. They can feel light touch, heavy pressure, heat and cold, vibrations, and pain.

VENUS'S-FLYTRAP
Small hairs on the two-part leaf feel the movements of a fly or similar victim. The leaf then closes and digests its meal.

Fly touches hairs

Leaf traps fly

HUMAN SKIN
This magnified view shows the pressure sensors, which signal that the skin is being pressed hard.

Pressure sensor in dermis

Petals open in sun

Petals close in rain

PLANTS
In some flowers, the petals open in sunshine. If spattered with rain, they close to protect the delicate flower parts.

WARM-BLOODED ANIMALS
Mammals and birds have sensors that monitor and regulate body temperature.

Bush baby has constant body temperature

Lizard warms up in sun

Lizard cools off in shade

COLD-BLOODED ANIMALS
Reptiles such as lizards bask in the sun to get warm. When too hot they cool off in the shade.

TIME
A crab kept in a tank with constant conditions, lacking tides or daylight and night, is still active on a tidal (12-hour) rhythm. Many animals and plants show such biorhythms, which coordinate their bodies and their behavior patterns with the most important changes in the environment.

Oak tree—annual

Crab—tidal

Migrating goose—annual

NERVES, BRAINS, AND BEHAVIOR

Every second, an animal's eyes, ears, and other sense organs produce millions of nerve signals. These tiny blips of electricity represent a wealth of information about the processes inside the animal's body, and also the events in the world around. In simpler animals this data passes into a network of nerves. An incoming nerve signal triggers a certain kind of reaction. For example, if an open sea anemone is prodded, it draws in its tentacles. In more complicated animals the signals are sent along nerves to the brain. The brain is the body's control center—a web of nerve cells, more intricate than the latest computer. Inside the brain, signals from the senses are gathered, compared, processed, and stored as necessary. The brain also sends out signals to the muscles. The outgoing signals produce patterns of movement and activities known as "behavior."

NERVE CELLS AND SYSTEMS

The basis of any nervous system is the nerve cell, or neuron. It sends tiny pulses of electricity along its thin, wire-like axon, which may stretch from one part of the body to another. A small worm's nervous system is relatively simple, with only a few thousand nerve cells. The octopus has the most complex system of any invertebrate; its behavior is correspondingly intricate. Mammals such as humans and lions have the most complicated and adaptable behavior. They can learn new behavior patterns from past experiences.

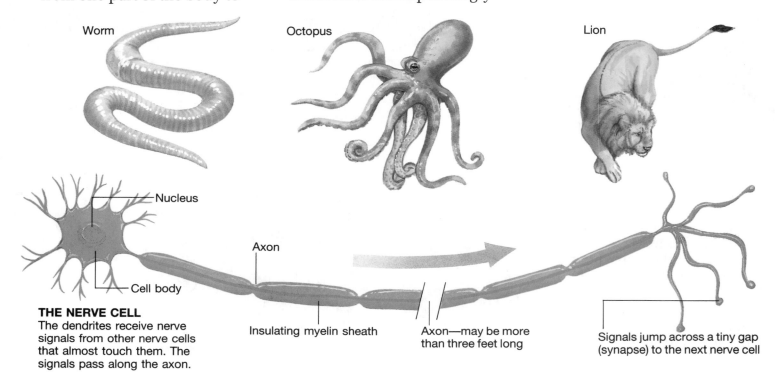

Worm

Octopus

Lion

Nucleus

Axon

Cell body

Insulating myelin sheath

Axon—may be more than three feet long

Signals jump across a tiny gap (synapse) to the next nerve cell

THE NERVE CELL
The dendrites receive nerve signals from other nerve cells that almost touch them. The signals pass along the axon.

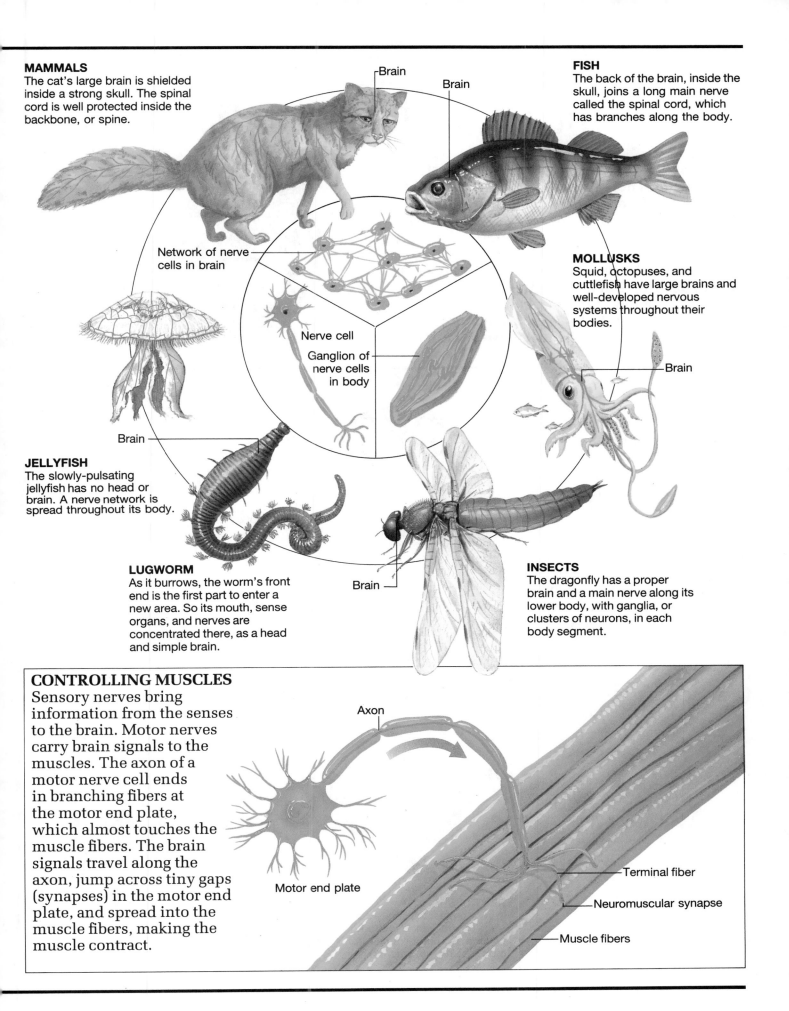

MAMMALS
The cat's large brain is shielded inside a strong skull. The spinal cord is well protected inside the backbone, or spine.

Brain

Brain

FISH
The back of the brain, inside the skull, joins a long main nerve called the spinal cord, which has branches along the body.

Network of nerve cells in brain

MOLLUSKS
Squid, octopuses, and cuttlefish have large brains and well-developed nervous systems throughout their bodies.

Brain

Nerve cell

Ganglion of nerve cells in body

JELLYFISH
The slowly-pulsating jellyfish has no head or brain. A nerve network is spread throughout its body.

Brain

LUGWORM
As it burrows, the worm's front end is the first part to enter a new area. So its mouth, sense organs, and nerves are concentrated there, as a head and simple brain.

Brain

INSECTS
The dragonfly has a proper brain and a main nerve along its lower body, with ganglia, or clusters of neurons, in each body segment.

CONTROLLING MUSCLES
Sensory nerves bring information from the senses to the brain. Motor nerves carry brain signals to the muscles. The axon of a motor nerve cell ends in branching fibers at the motor end plate, which almost touches the muscle fibers. The brain signals travel along the axon, jump across tiny gaps (synapses) in the motor end plate, and spread into the muscle fibers, making the muscle contract.

Axon

Motor end plate

Terminal fiber

Neuromuscular synapse

Muscle fibers

BIGGER BRAINS

Unlike a pumping heart or squirming intestines, the brain does not move. Its activities are at the microscopic level—pulses of electricity flash around its vast network of nerve cells. The brain controls and coordinates, continually assessing the input from the senses and deciding which muscles to order into action. In our own bodies, we are not aware of many of the brain's activities. It makes the heart beat, the lungs breathe, and the intestines push food through them, automatically, even when we fall asleep.

BRAIN PARTS
In the animal world there are various designs of brains, each with abilities suited to the owner's way of life. The brain's various lobes, or bulges, deal with different aspects of sensory information, processing and movements. For example, the olfactory lobes process signals from the smell organs, and they are large in animals that depend heavily on the sense of smell. Optic lobes deal with signals from the eyes.

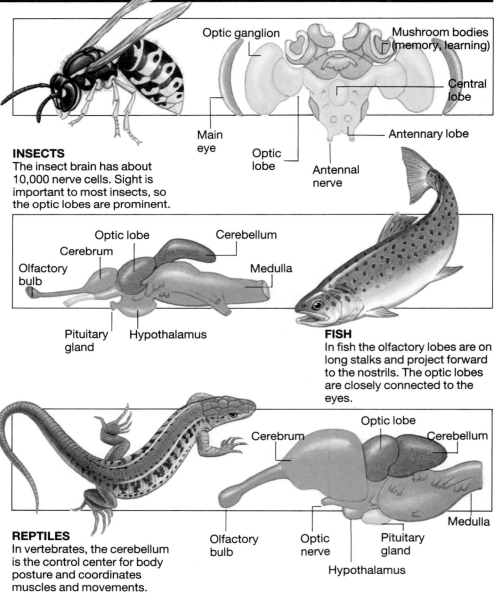

INSECTS
The insect brain has about 10,000 nerve cells. Sight is important to most insects, so the optic lobes are prominent.

Labels: Optic ganglion; Mushroom bodies (memory, learning); Central lobe; Antennary lobe; Main eye; Optic lobe; Antennal nerve

FISH
In fish the olfactory lobes are on long stalks and project forward to the nostrils. The optic lobes are closely connected to the eyes.

Labels: Optic lobe; Cerebellum; Cerebrum; Olfactory bulb; Medulla; Pituitary gland; Hypothalamus

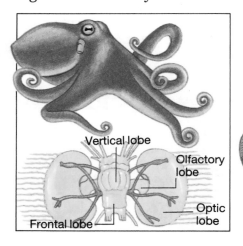

OCTOPUS
This large, complex brain has 15 main pairs of lobes and an extra nerve ring to help control muscles in the eight arms.

Labels: Vertical lobe; Olfactory lobe; Optic lobe; Frontal lobe

REPTILES
In vertebrates, the cerebellum is the control center for body posture and coordinates muscles and movements.

Labels: Optic lobe; Cerebrum; Cerebellum; Olfactory bulb; Optic nerve; Pituitary gland; Hypothalamus; Medulla

64

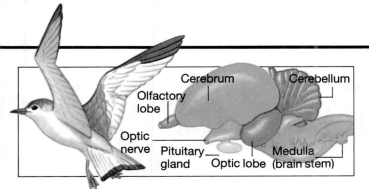

Cerebrum **Cerebellum**
Olfactory lobe
Optic nerve
Pituitary gland
Optic lobe
Medulla (brain stem)

BIRD

Most birds have huge optic lobes, showing how sight dominates their lives. They can see clearly, even in dim conditions, and, like us, can distinguish different colors. The cerebellum, which coordinates complex muscle movements, is also well developed. The olfactory lobes are small, and it is thought that some birds can hardly smell at all.

Cerebrum **Cerebellum**
Olfactory lobe
Optic nerve
Medulla

MAMMALS

The cerebrum is large in mammals, forming most of the brain. Grooves and bulges increase its surface area. It receives sensory information from the skin, face, and limbs, and sends out signals to move these parts.

BRAIN AND BODY

The biggest brains are not necessarily the cleverest. The largest animal brain of all is that of the sperm whale. It weighs over 20 pounds, compared to an average human brain at 3 pounds. A more useful indicator of intelligence is the comparison between the ratio of brain size to body size, shown here for several different mammals.

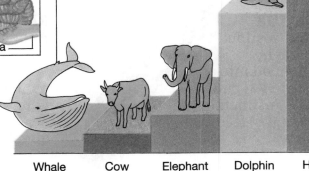

Whale   Cow   Elephant   Dolphin   Human

THINKING

The frontal lobes are involved in memories, thoughts, emotions, and "personality"—though exactly how is not clear.

MOVING

Signals are sent from the motor center, via the cerebellum, to the muscles of the face, body, and limbs.

THE HUMAN BRAIN

The largest part of the human brain is the cerebrum, where memory, thought, and reasoning are based. It is divided into two hemispheres. Its various "centers" have specific functions.

TOUCHING

Each part of the body's sensory center processes signals coming from the skin on a corresponding part of the body.

COORDINATION

The cerebellum is a two-lobed area that organizes signals sent to the muscles to coordinate body movements.

CEREBRAL COMPLEXITY

A piece of cerebrum one millimeter square and two millimeters thick contains about 60,000 nerve cells. And each of these nerve cells is connected to more than 50,000 others!

HEARING

Nerve signals from the ears are sorted out here, then passed to other areas of the cerebrum for deciphering.

SEEING

The optic lobe located at the rear of the cerebrum analyzes nerve signals from the eyes and forms a mental picture of what we see.

SIMPLE BEHAVIOR

The scientific study of animal behavior is called ethology. It is a very complicated subject. Even in simple animals, the "wiring" of the brain and nervous system within each body is unique, so the response to a certain situation may vary from one individual to the next. In more complicated animals, behavior also depends on past experiences and what the animal has learned and remembered. Several straightforward types of behavior are shown here. Some are automatic; others can be changed by learning.

BUILT-IN BEHAVIOR

Sometimes called "instinct," this is behavior that is somehow programmed into an animal's genes (page 73) and is present from birth. Instincts help the baby animal to feed and survive.

REFLEX

A reflex is a movement that occurs without the animal "thinking" about it. If your hand touches a hot object, your body's reflex is to pull away at once, even if your attention is elsewhere.

Chick pecks at mother's beak

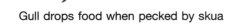

Gull drops food when pecked by skua

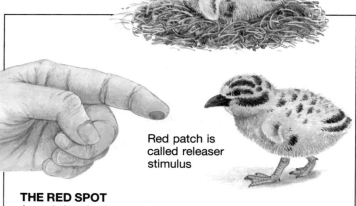

Red patch is called releaser stimulus

THE RED SPOT

A newly hatched sea gull pecks at its mother's beak so that she will feed it. Tests demonstrate that the chick pecks instinctively at any red spot.

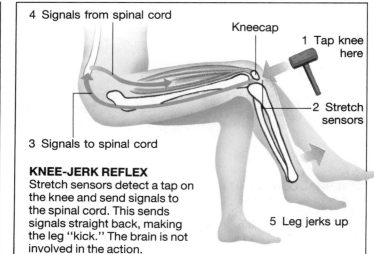

4 Signals from spinal cord

Kneecap

1 Tap knee here

2 Stretch sensors

3 Signals to spinal cord

5 Leg jerks up

KNEE-JERK REFLEX

Stretch sensors detect a tap on the knee and send signals to the spinal cord. This sends signals straight back, making the leg "kick." The brain is not involved in the action.

HABITUATION

A fanworm responds to being touched by pulling its feathery tentacles down into its tube. This is a defensive action. But if it is touched many times, the fanworm no longer responds. It "gets used to" a stimulus that is not dangerous, and it no longer reacts in the usual way. This process is called habituation.

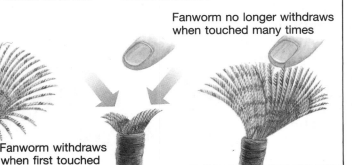

Fanworm no longer withdraws when touched many times

Fanworm withdraws when first touched

LEARNING

A sea gull looking for food eats the leftovers from a fishing boat. Next time it sees a boat, it recalls the link between the boat and food. This is an example of learning—acquiring new behavior from experience and memory.

Gull associates sight of boat with food

Other gulls notice and copy the behavior

ALTERING REFLEXES

When a dog sees and smells food, its mouth waters automatically. This is the salivating reflex. In an experiment conducted by Russian biologist Ivan Pavlov, every time a dog was fed, a bell was rung.

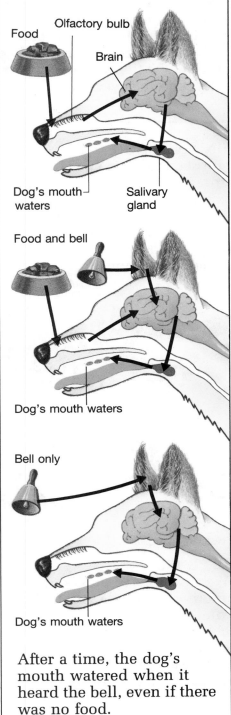

Food

Olfactory bulb

Brain

Dog's mouth waters

Salivary gland

Food and bell

Dog's mouth waters

Bell only

Dog's mouth waters

After a time, the dog's mouth watered when it heard the bell, even if there was no food.

COMPLEX BEHAVIOR

Animals combine their many types of simple behavior patterns to produce the activities of daily life. Some are able to integrate learned activities with automatic ones, and continually adapt their behavior. A squirrel learns where to bite different types of nuts so that they split open easily. Behavior patterns are designed to aid survival, and they can be named according to their main purpose, such as feeding, escaping, or nesting. Yet they are all still controlled by nerve cells carrying nerve signals.

FINDING FOOD
The need to eat is one of the strongest "feelings" an animal experiences. Basic urges such as hunger, which bring about behavior patterns even if there is no outside stimulus, are called motivations.

Cobra spreads hood

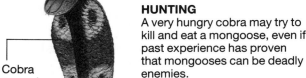

HUNTING
A very hungry cobra may try to kill and eat a mongoose, even if past experience has proven that mongooses can be deadly enemies.

PASSIVE FEEDING
The barnacle, cousin of the crab, gathers tiny bits of floating food by kicking them into its mouth with its feathery limbs. Many sea creatures, such as mussels and sea lilies, filter-feed in this way.

Hard protective shell

PUSS MOTH CATERPILLAR
If in danger, this caterpillar rears up and shows its red head, waves its long "tails," and squirts methanoic (formic) acid. Its behavior startles and repels many predators.

HEDGEHOG
This prickly mammal tucks in its head and legs when threatened, forming a ball of spines that few predators can penetrate.

Resting caterpillar   Caterpillar in defense posture

DEFENSE
Warding off enemies is another basic behavior that is vital for survival. This behavior may rely on displaying part of the body to surprise or frighten the attacker, or presenting defensive horns, spines, or prickles.

Head tucked in

Hedgehog rolls into ball

ESCAPING

An alternative to on-the-spot defense is to flee or escape. The creature must be able to outpace or outmaneuver its attacker, or quickly get into a burrow, crack, or other place where the attacker cannot follow.

Worm pulls into burrow if touched

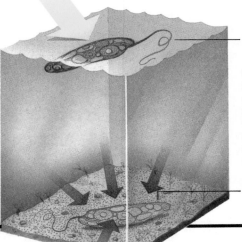

MOTH
Some moths can hear the high-pitched "sound radar" of a hunting bat. They escape either by zigzagging or by flying straight down.

Moth hears bat's sonar

Moth escapes by zigzag flight

Moth escapes by power dive

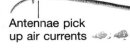

Antennae pick up air currents

EARTHWORM
Worms may come to the surface, especially to breed. If they feel vibrations or touch, they rapidly withdraw back into their burrows.

Sunlight

COCKROACH
Air currents warn a cockroach of approaching danger, and it quickly runs and hides in a crack under a floorboard.

Dry and dark

AVOIDING BAD CONDITIONS

Only a few animals, such as those at the bottom of the sea, live in an unchanging world. Most creatures have to move around to avoid unsuitable conditions, as the environment changes with the days and seasons.

Experiment box

PROTISTS
Some microscopic water-dwellers move near the surface during the day, to get the best light for photosynthesis. At night they sink to the bottom and absorb food, like animals.

Dry and light

WOOD LICE
Given a choice of conditions, wood lice congregate in a dark, damp place. Otherwise they would dry out and die.

Damp and light

Damp and dark

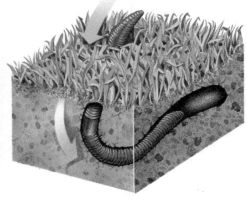

Photosynthesis near surface

SWALLOWS
Some creatures avoid bad conditions by migrating to more suitable places. They remember their nest sites and fly back to them each year. Other animals hibernate until conditions improve.

Feeding in deeper water

Swallows gather before migration

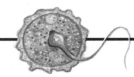

REPRODUCTION

One of the oldest questions is: Why are we here? Not only why are humans here, but other animals too? Why do they struggle to survive, find food, and fight off enemies? And why are plants here? One answer is to reproduce, to make more of their kind. Although there is a great variety of life forms on Earth, there are only a few basic methods of reproduction. Some organisms produce offspring by themselves; this is called asexual reproduction. Others get together in some way with another of their species, in the process called sexual reproduction.

The time scale of reproduction varies greatly. Every few hours a bacterium splits in half and forms two "daughters." Every year, sparrow chicks hatch from eggs laid by their mother. Every five years, a female elephant bears a baby which has been developing in her womb for almost two years.

ASEXUAL REPRODUCTION
This is reproduction by a single creature or plant without a sexual partner. It is common in smaller, simpler organisms.

SPORES
These tiny structures play a major role in the reproduction of some protozoans and many plants and fungi. Some spores are produced asexually; others are formed during sexual reproduction.

PROTISTS
A simple, single-celled protist such as an amoeba splits in two by the process of cell division or mitosis (page 74).

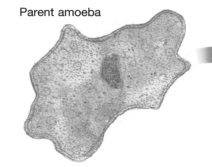

Parent amoeba

Cell divides

Two daughter amoebae

FERN
Ferns produce spores, which form in little capsules on the underside of their leaves (fronds) and are blown away by the wind.

FUNGI
Some fungi such as mushrooms and toadstools grow spore-making parts, which release millions of microscopic spores.

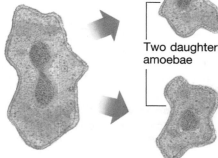

Mushroom spores scatter in wind

Fern spores scatter in wind

SEXUAL REPRODUCTION

In sexual reproduction, two parents make the offspring. Usually, the female parent produces an egg cell. The male parent produces a male sex cell (in animals, a sperm cell) to fertilize, or join with, the egg cell.

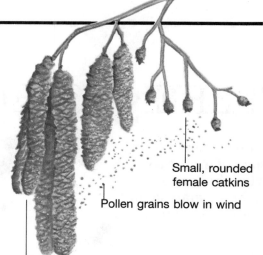

TREE CATKINS
Male catkins make pollen grains which contain male sex cells. These blow in the wind to the female catkins, which contain egg cells.

Small, rounded female catkins

Pollen grains blow in wind

Long, feathery male catkins

Sperms and eggs released into water

SEA URCHIN
Many sea creatures release their eggs and sperms into the water. These float around and come together by chance. Sea water is a "soup" of millions of eggs and sperms from all manner of animals.

Gonad (sex organ)

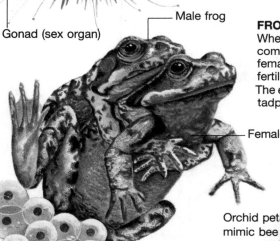

Male frog

FROG
When a male and female frog come together and mate, as the female lays the eggs, the male fertilizes them with his sperm. The eggs then develop to form tadpoles.

Female frog

Orchid petals mimic bee

Female lays eggs (called spawn)

BEE ORCHID
The pollen grains containing male cells of one bee orchid must get to the female parts of another. The orchid looks like a bee, and bees try to mate with it. The pollen grains stick to the bee, who carries them to another bee orchid flower.

PARENTAL CARE

In some animals, when the young hatch or are born, the parents take care of them and help them to survive and grow. Parental care occurs in many birds and mammals and in a few insects and other invertebrates.

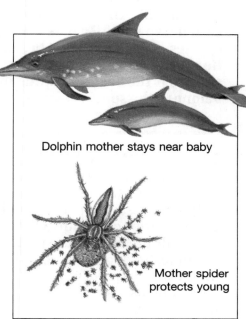

Dolphin mother stays near baby

Mother spider protects young

FAST BREEDING

In the summer a female aphid is able to produce young without mating with a male. Development of egg cells into young like this, without fertilization, is called parthenogenesis.

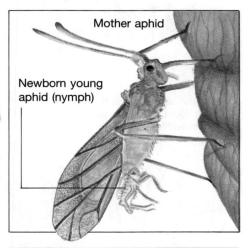

Mother aphid

Newborn young aphid (nymph)

DIFFERENT SPECIES

When animals and plants reproduce sexually they can do so only with partners of their own kind. And they produce offspring that are also of their own kind. For example, when a male jackal mates with a female jackal she gives birth to a baby jackal. All jackals belong to one large unit called a species. Hyenas belong to another species. A jackal cannot breed with a hyena, or a lion, or a member of any other species. The species is the basic grouping in nature. We belong to the species *Homo sapiens*.

German shepherd

RECOGNIZING SPECIES

In general, all members of a species look similar. It is easy to tell apart some species, such as dogs from cats. But what about all the different varieties of domestic dogs? The fact that they can all breed with each other means they belong to the same species.

Beagle

Poodle

DOGS
Over many years, dog breeders have produced different breeds, or varieties, of the single species of domestic dog.

Carp

Dalmatian

FISH
To our eyes some fish species look almost identical to each other. But fish always recognize and breed with members of their own species.

Rainbow trout

Goldfish

INTERBREEDING

Sometimes members from different species mate and produce young. A lion and tiger may mate, and the baby "tigon" looks like a mixture of both parents. But it is a hybrid (see opposite) and cannot breed because it is infertile.

ORANGUTAN
A female orangutan is much smaller than a male. But because they are of the same species, their offspring grow up fertile (able to breed).

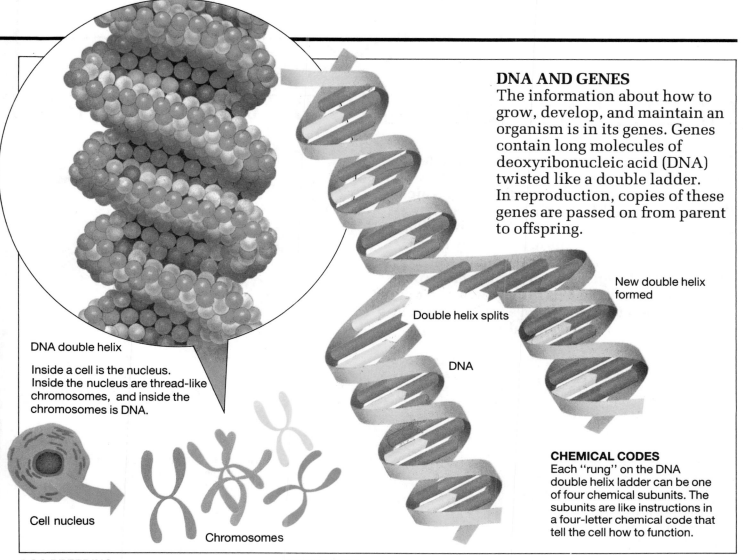

DNA AND GENES
The information about how to grow, develop, and maintain an organism is in its genes. Genes contain long molecules of deoxyribonucleic acid (DNA) twisted like a double ladder. In reproduction, copies of these genes are passed on from parent to offspring.

DNA double helix

Inside a cell is the nucleus. Inside the nucleus are thread-like chromosomes, and inside the chromosomes is DNA.

Cell nucleus

Chromosomes

New double helix formed

Double helix splits

DNA

CHEMICAL CODES
Each "rung" on the DNA double helix ladder can be one of four chemical subunits. The subunits are like instructions in a four-letter chemical code that tell the cell how to function.

DOG BREEDING
When two breeds of dog mate, the puppies may have a combination of features from each parent. The puppies are called crossbreeds.

Labrador

Smooth collie

Crossbreed puppies

HYBRIDS
The offspring of parents from different species is a hybrid. Hybrids cannot make eggs or sperms because the pieces of DNA they inherit from each parent do not match.

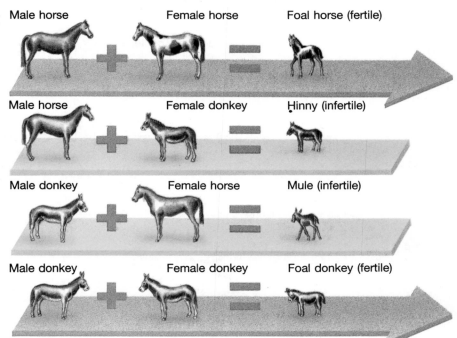

Male horse + Female horse = Foal horse (fertile)

Male horse + Female donkey = Hinny (infertile)

Male donkey + Female horse = Mule (infertile)

Male donkey + Female donkey = Foal donkey (fertile)

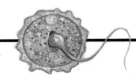

CELL DIVISION AND DEVELOPMENT

In sexual reproduction, a male cell from the father fertilizes an egg cell from the mother. The result is a single cell—the fertilized egg, which is the start of a new life. Further growth and development occurs when the first cell divides and then subsequent cells divide many times. This type of cell division is called mitosis. Eventually cells specialize to form organs (page 23). When the organism is fully grown and ready to reproduce it makes its own eggs or sperms by a special kind of cell division called meiosis.

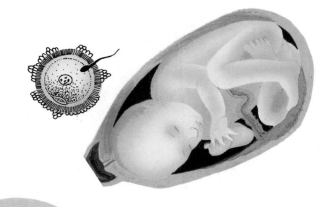

MITOSIS

During mitosis, pairs of gene-carrying chromosomes from the nucleus line up across the middle of the cell. The members of each pair move to opposite ends of the cell. The cell membrane pinches in two, making two separate daughter cells. A daughter cell has only one chromosome from each original pair. As it grows, the DNA in each chromosome copies itself, creating a duplicate set of chromosomes ready for the next division. A new nucleus develops in each of the new cells.

1 Chromosomes change from long, thin threads to thicker coils

Daughter cells begin to grow to size of mother cell

4 Cell pinched in two

2 Chromosomes line up in center of cell

3 Members of each chromosome pair move apart

STRAWBERRY PLANT

Asexual reproduction involves mitosis and cell differentiation, which produces structures such as the strawberry plant's runners. It uses the runners to create copies of itself.

HYDRA

The hydra buds by mitosis. Its offspring has the same chromosomes, and so the same genes, as its parent.

Daughter hydra buds off parent

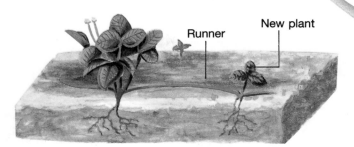

Runner

New plant

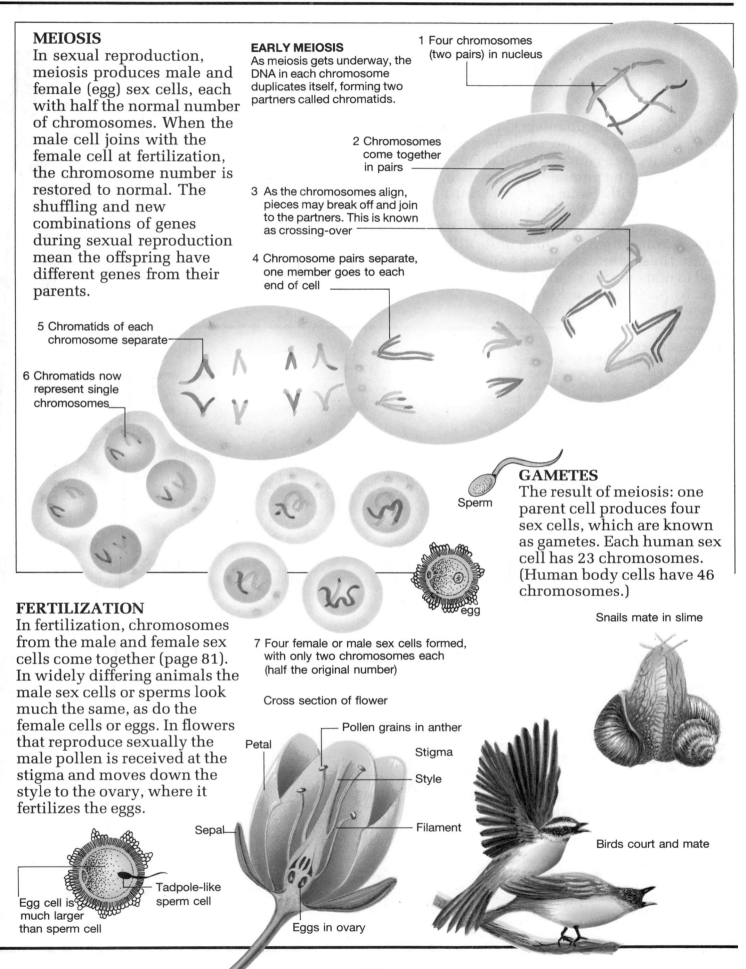

MEIOSIS

In sexual reproduction, meiosis produces male and female (egg) sex cells, each with half the normal number of chromosomes. When the male cell joins with the female cell at fertilization, the chromosome number is restored to normal. The shuffling and new combinations of genes during sexual reproduction mean the offspring have different genes from their parents.

EARLY MEIOSIS
As meiosis gets underway, the DNA in each chromosome duplicates itself, forming two partners called chromatids.

1 Four chromosomes (two pairs) in nucleus

2 Chromosomes come together in pairs

3 As the chromosomes align, pieces may break off and join to the partners. This is known as crossing-over

4 Chromosome pairs separate, one member goes to each end of cell

5 Chromatids of each chromosome separate

6 Chromatids now represent single chromosomes

Sperm

GAMETES

The result of meiosis: one parent cell produces four sex cells, which are known as gametes. Each human sex cell has 23 chromosomes. (Human body cells have 46 chromosomes.)

egg

FERTILIZATION

In fertilization, chromosomes from the male and female sex cells come together (page 81). In widely differing animals the male sex cells or sperms look much the same, as do the female cells or eggs. In flowers that reproduce sexually the male pollen is received at the stigma and moves down the style to the ovary, where it fertilizes the eggs.

7 Four female or male sex cells formed, with only two chromosomes each (half the original number)

Cross section of flower

Egg cell is much larger than sperm cell

Tadpole-like sperm cell

Sepal

Petal

Pollen grains in anther

Stigma

Style

Filament

Eggs in ovary

Snails mate in slime

Birds court and mate

75

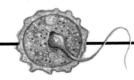

LIFE CYCLES 1

The life cycle of an organism shows how it grows from a fertilized egg into a mature adult, and then produces its own young. Not all plants and animals have the human-type life history that we are familiar with: being born, growing up, mating, and having young. Many plants and animals have two or more distinct phases in their lives, during which they look quite different. At certain times, animals such as aphids do not even need to mate. Each female produces young on her own, by parthenogenesis (page 71).

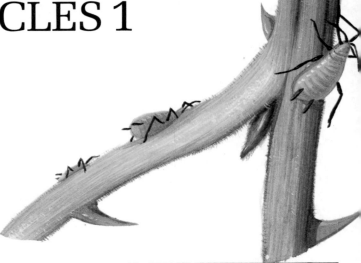

ALGAE (SEAWEEDS)
The large frond is called the sporophyte stage. It produces microscopic spores. Each spore grows into either a male plant that makes male sex cells or a female plant that makes eggs. These are gametophyte stages.

MOSSES
The main moss plant is the gametophyte. Its fertilized egg cells grow into "swan-necked" sporangia, the sporophyte stage—which release thousands of spores. These blow away and grow into new moss plants.

LIVERWORTS
As in mosses, the main liverwort plant is the gametophyte stage, and its cells have half the number of chromosomes of the sporophtye stage. The gametophyte makes male sex cells and eggs by mitosis.

JELLYFISH
Sea anemones, jellyfish and corals belong to a group of animals called coelenterates. The jellyfish has a two-stage life cycle, one being the free-swimming medusa, and the other the anchored-down polyp.

ROUNDWORMS
Some roundworms, or nematodes, are parasites. They steal nutrients from the host animal. The *Ascaris* roundworm in a pig is a good example. Its life cycle is designed to get the eggs rapidly into another host.

EARTHWORMS
Each earthworm is a hermaphrodite, which means it has both male and female sex organs, and so it can make sperms and eggs. At mating, each worm passes its sperms to the partner.

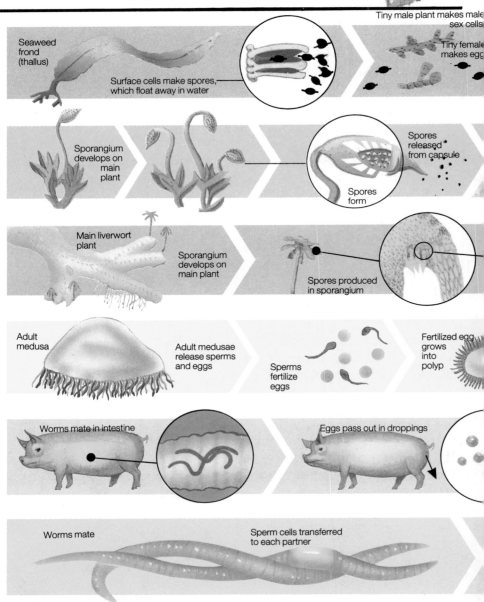

Tiny male plant makes male sex cells

Seaweed frond (thallus)

Surface cells make spores, which float away in water

Tiny female makes eggs

Sporangium develops on main plant

Spores released from capsule

Spores form

Main liverwort plant

Sporangium develops on main plant

Spores produced in sporangium

Adult medusa

Adult medusae release sperms and eggs

Sperms fertilize eggs

Fertilized egg grows into polyp

Worms mate in intestine

Eggs pass out in droppings

Worms mate

Sperm cells transferred to each partner

SEA ANEMONE

The sea anemone is a close relative of the jellyfish (below). But unlike the jellyfish with its medusa and polyp phases, the anemone has virtually a one-stage lifecycle, which corresponds to the jellyfish polyp. Sex cells are made in the gonads, or reproductive organs, in the anemone's stomach cavity. These cells are ejected into the water, where by chance they encounter sex cells from other anemones. Some anemones can also reproduce asexually.

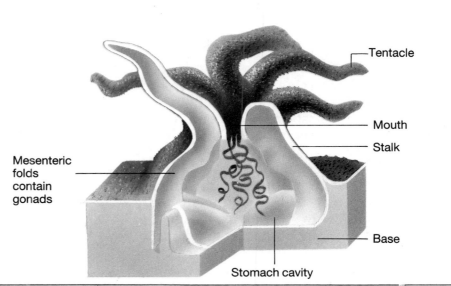

Tentacle

Mouth

Stalk

Mesenteric folds contain gonads

Base

Stomach cavity

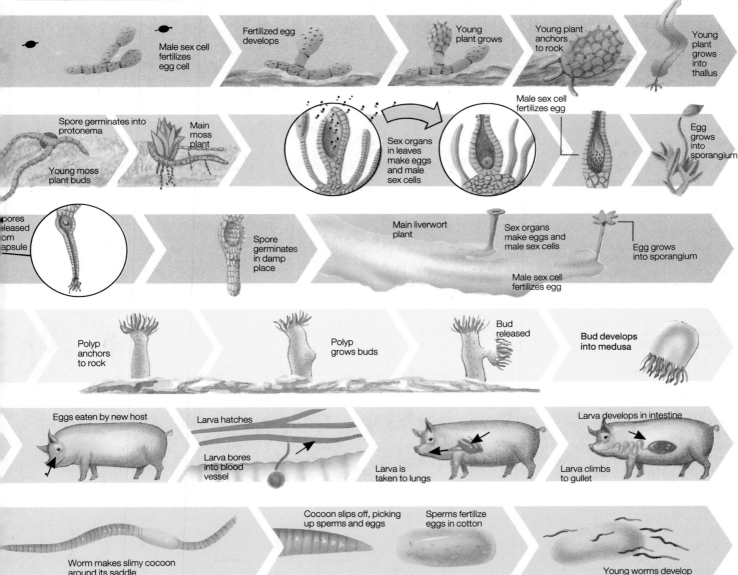

Male sex cell fertilizes egg cell

Fertilized egg develops

Young plant grows

Young plant anchors to rock

Young plant grows into thallus

Spore germinates into protonema

Young moss plant buds

Main moss plant

Sex organs in leaves make eggs and male sex cells

Male sex cell fertilizes egg

Egg grows into sporangium

Spores released from capsule

Spore germinates in damp place

Main liverwort plant

Sex organs make eggs and male sex cells

Male sex cell fertilizes egg

Egg grows into sporangium

Polyp anchors to rock

Polyp grows buds

Bud released

Bud develops into medusa

Eggs eaten by new host

Larva hatches

Larva bores into blood vessel

Larva is taken to lungs

Larva climbs to gullet

Larva develops in intestine

Worm makes slimy cocoon around its saddle

Cocoon slips off, picking up sperms and eggs

Sperms fertilize eggs in cotton

Young worms develop and hatch from cocoon

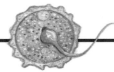

LIFE CYCLES 2

Knowing about each stage in the life cycle of a plant or animal is very important. If you discovered for the first time a caterpillar munching on a leaf and a butterfly sipping nectar from a flower, you might decide they were two different kinds of animals. But watch for long enough: the caterpillar (larva) would change into a chrysalis (pupa), then into a butterfly. Only by studying an organism through every phase of its life cycles, can we piece together the correct life history for each living thing.

FERNS
Like the moss and liverwort, ferns show "alternation of generations"—the sporophyte stage alternates with the gametophyte stage. The main fern plant is the sporophyte.

STARFISH
In most starfish species, males and females cast their eggs and sperms into the sea at about the same time. A fertilized egg passes through several larval stages before becoming an adult.

BUTTERFLIES
This type of insect goes through complete metamorphosis (page 47). The female mates with a male and lays fertilized eggs. The eggs hatch into larvae, which change into pupae before becoming adults.

SPIDERS
In most spider species the male is much smaller than the female. He must be very careful in his courting behavior before mating—if his partner is hungry she may bite and kill him!

SALMON
In the salmon, male and female come together after their exhausting journey up-river. She lays her eggs in the gravel in a streambed, and he squirts sperms over them. The whole process is known as spawning.

DOGFISH
When mating, the male dogfish swims near the female, twines around her body, and passes his sperm into her body using his claspers. She lays tough egg cases in which the embryos develop.

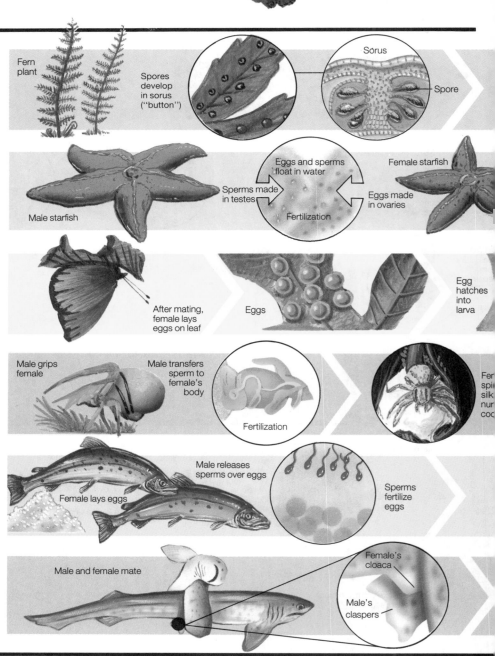

Fern plant

Spores develop in sorus ("button")

Sorus

Spore

Male starfish

Sperms made in testes

Eggs and sperms float in water

Fertilization

Female starfish

Eggs made in ovaries

After mating, female lays eggs on leaf

Eggs

Egg hatches into larva

Male grips female

Male transfers sperm to female's body

Fertilization

Fer spi silk nur coc

Female lays eggs

Male releases sperms over eggs

Sperms fertilize eggs

Male and female mate

Female's cloaca

Male's claspers

SNAIL

Like the earthworm on page 76, a typical snail is a hermaphrodite. It has both male and female sex organs combined in one body part called the ovotestis or hermaphrodite gland, which produces sperms as well as eggs. When two snails mate they become stimulated by spearing each other with tiny, chalky "love darts"; they twine around each other in a mass of frothy slime, then exchange sperm packets. Each one then goes off to lay its eggs.

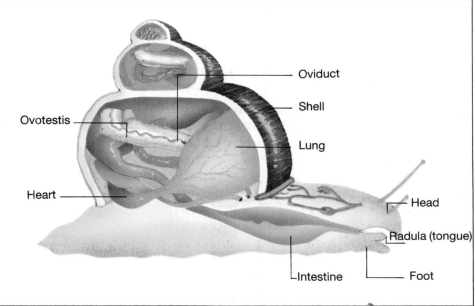

Oviduct

Shell

Ovotestis

Lung

Heart

Head

Radula (tongue)

Intestine

Foot

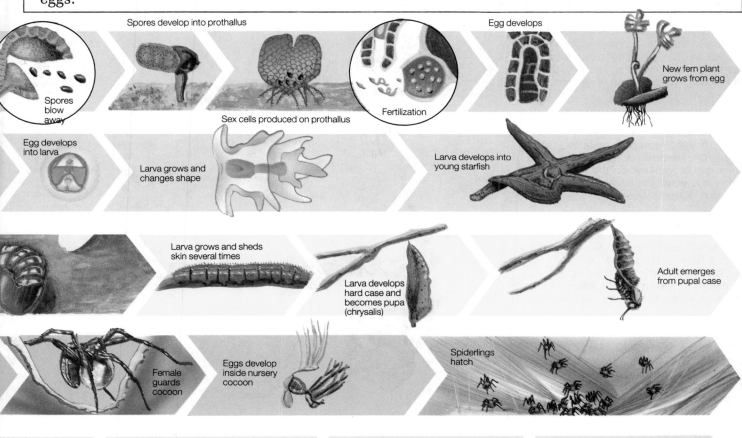

Spores develop into prothallus

Egg develops

Spores blow away

Sex cells produced on prothallus

Fertilization

New fern plant grows from egg

Egg develops into larva

Larva grows and changes shape

Larva develops into young starfish

Larva grows and sheds skin several times

Larva develops hard case and becomes pupa (chrysalis)

Adult emerges from pupal case

Female guards cocoon

Eggs develop inside nursery cocoon

Spiderlings hatch

Embryo fish develop in eggs

Young fish (fry)

Yolk for food

Fry grows and can feed itself

Fry develops into adult

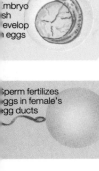

Sperm fertilizes eggs in female's egg ducts

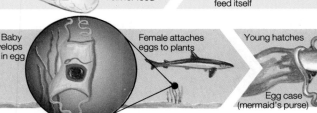

Baby develops in egg

Female attaches eggs to plants

Young hatches

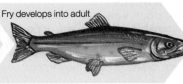

Young dogfish feeds and grows

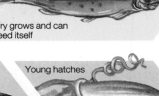

Egg case (mermaid's purse)

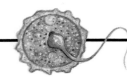

LIFE CYCLES 3

In the plant kingdom the reproductive parts reach their greatest complexity and beauty in the flowers of trees and other flowering plants. Many of these plants enlist the help of bees, bats, birds, and other creatures to transfer their pollen from one to another. This is called pollination. Animals such as birds and mammals have complicated courtship and mating behavior. This behavior helps each pair to ensure they have chosen a mate of the same species who is ready to breed and who is fit, strong, and healthy.

PINE TREES
In seed-bearing plants the main plant is the sporophyte stage. A pine produces female cones containing egg cells, and male cones containing pollen. The wind blows the pollen, which pollinates the female cones.

FLOWERS
Many flowers have both male and female parts. But various mechanisms, such as a time gap between when the male parts ripen and when the female ones are ready, prevent self-pollination.

SNAKES
Some snakes are oviparous—after mating with a male the female lays eggs containing the developing young. A few snakes are viviparous—the babies develop in the mother and are born fully formed.

BIRDS
All birds lay eggs. Each contains a large amount of yolk which nourishes the developing chick. Bird parents must keep their eggs warm so they can develop, a process called incubation.

MARSUPIALS
Kangaroos, koalas, wombats, and similar mammals are marsupials, or pouched mammals. The young are born early in development, tiny and helpless. They develop and grow in the mother's pouch.

HUMAN
Cats, dogs, horses, humans, and most other mammals are placental mammals. This means a baby develops inside its mother's womb and a special part, the placenta, transfers nourishment from mother to baby.

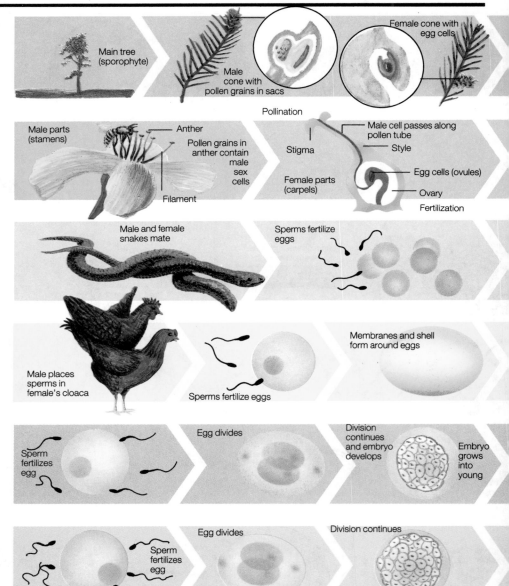

Main tree (sporophyte)

Male cone with pollen grains in sacs

Female cone with egg cells

Pollination

Male parts (stamens)

Anther

Pollen grains in anther contain male sex cells

Filament

Stigma

Female parts (carpels)

Male cell passes along pollen tube

Style

Egg cells (ovules)

Ovary

Fertilization

Male and female snakes mate

Sperms fertilize eggs

Male places sperms in female's cloaca

Sperms fertilize eggs

Membranes and shell form around eggs

Sperm fertilizes egg

Egg divides

Division continues and embryo develops

Embryo grows into young

Sperm fertilizes egg

Egg divides

Division continues

PLACENTAL MAMMAL

In a placental mammal such as a cat, the placenta is embedded in the wall of the womb (uterus). The baby is attached to it by the umbilical cord. The baby's blood, which circulates throughout its body, flows along the cord to the placenta to pick up oxygen and nutrients from the mother's blood (the two blood systems do not mix). The baby's blood also passes wastes to the mother's blood. The blood then flows back along the cord and into the baby's body.

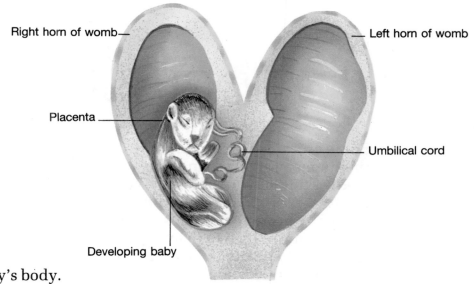

Right horn of womb

Left horn of womb

Placenta

Umbilical cord

Developing baby

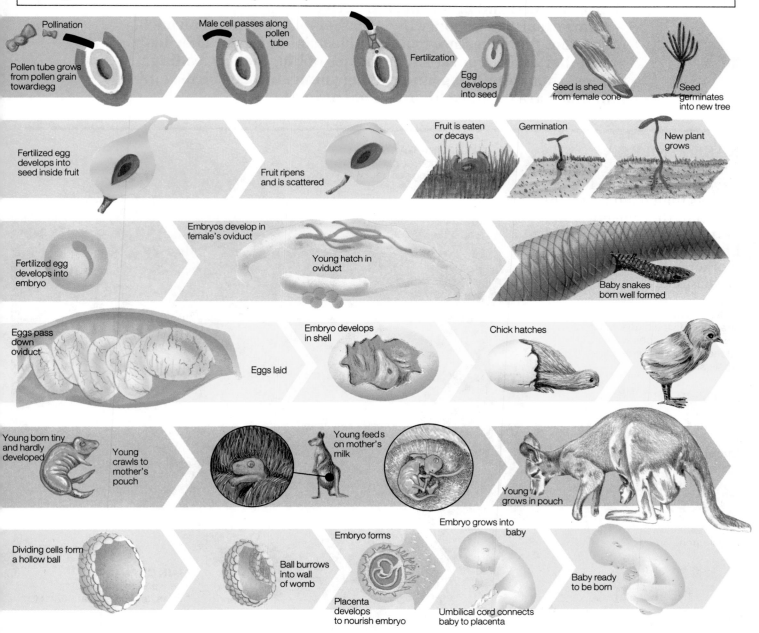

Pollination

Pollen tube grows from pollen grain toward egg

Male cell passes along pollen tube

Fertilization

Egg develops into seed

Seed is shed from female cone

Seed germinates into new tree

Fertilized egg develops into seed inside fruit

Fruit ripens and is scattered

Fruit is eaten or decays

Germination

New plant grows

Fertilized egg develops into embryo

Embryos develop in female's oviduct

Young hatch in oviduct

Baby snakes born well formed

Eggs pass down oviduct

Eggs laid

Embryo develops in shell

Chick hatches

Young born tiny and hardly developed

Young crawls to mother's pouch

Young feeds on mother's milk

Young grows in pouch

Dividing cells form a hollow ball

Ball burrows into wall of womb

Embryo forms

Placenta develops to nourish embryo

Embryo grows into baby

Umbilical cord connects baby to placenta

Baby ready to be born

SOCIALIZING

Some animals live on their own. They only encounter others of their species at breeding time. Otherwise they live alone, feeding and hiding and surviving without help from their fellows. Worms, starfish, slugs, and salamanders are a few of the many animals that follow the life of a loner.

Other animals live in groups. Tuna swim in schools, and starlings fly in flocks. Animals like these could probably survive on their own. But in a large group they find safety, and they often feed and breed more effectively.

Some creatures not only live together—they depend on each other, too. They are known as highly social animals. They help each other and cooperate in the basics of life, such as feeding, defense, home-building, and raising young. Insects, birds, and mammals are the most highly social animals.

NAKED MOLE RAT

These strange African rodents have a society more like insects than mammals. Only one pair, the "queen" and "king," produces young. Most of the colony members are workers; they dig tunnels and gather food.

NAKED MOLE RAT SIZES
The queen is the biggest colony member. She is looked after by attendants. The workers are smallest.

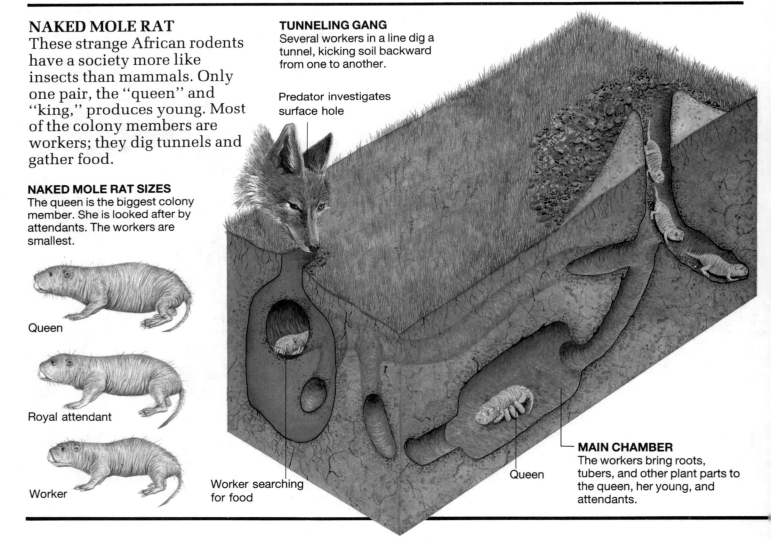

Queen

Royal attendant

Worker

TUNNELING GANG
Several workers in a line dig a tunnel, kicking soil backward from one to another.

Predator investigates surface hole

Worker searching for food

Queen

MAIN CHAMBER
The workers bring roots, tubers, and other plant parts to the queen, her young, and attendants.

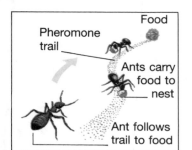

THE ANT'S FOOD TRAIL
If a foraging ant finds food it makes an invisible scent called a pheromone (page 60) in its body and lays a scent trail back to the nest. Other workers follow the trail to the food and carry it back to the colony.

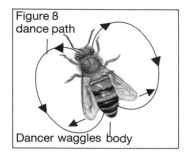

THE BEE'S FOOD DANCE
If a honey bee finds nectar-rich flowers it returns to the hive and does a figure of 8 dance on the comb. The position and angle of the 8, and the waggles of the bee's body, tell other workers where the food is.

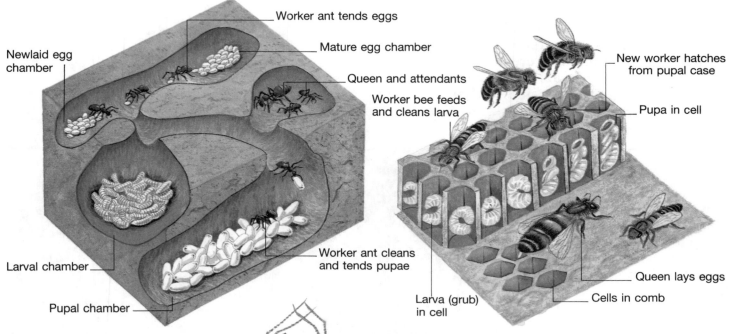

Worker ant tends eggs

Mature egg chamber

Queen and attendants

Worker bee feeds and cleans larva

Newlaid egg chamber

New worker hatches from pupal case

Pupa in cell

Larval chamber

Worker ant cleans and tends pupae

Pupal chamber

Larva (grub) in cell

Queen lays eggs

Cells in comb

INSIDE THE ANTS' NEST
Some ants live in soil or under piles of leaves and twigs. They dig a nest with different chambers for the developing young, as they pass through the egg, larval (grub), and pupal stages of the life cycle.

Ants communicate by tapping their antennae together

INSIDE THE BEES' HIVE
Honey bees, like ants, live in colonies, and each bee has its own job. Only the queen lays eggs. Workers clean the hive, bring food and water, and cool the hive in summer by fanning the air with their wings.

TYPES OF TERMITE
A termite colony may contain over a million termites. The huge queen lays thousands of eggs daily, attended by the king. Big-jawed soldiers defend the nest while workers collect food.

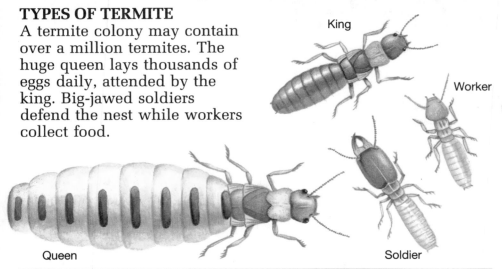

King

Worker

Queen

Soldier

Red spider mite   Earwig

Small centipede

Wood louse (sow bug)

NOT REALLY SOCIAL
Some animals seem social, but they are not. Small creatures gather under bark simply because it is a cool, damp place.

FAMILY LIFE

Birds and mammals commonly live in family groups, especially at breeding time. There are various combinations of parents and offspring. Often the group is just mother and young, as in ducks and foxes. In a few cases the father looks after the young, as in ostriches. The two-parent family is very common, in creatures from swans to beavers. Other animals live in extended families consisting of parents, newborns, sisters and brothers, aunts and uncles, and other relatives.

Baby cuckoo is raised by its foster family

THE GORILLA TROOP

Gorillas and chimps are our closest relatives in the animal world. An average gorilla troop has a large chief male, the silverback (named from the whitish-silver hair on his back), with 2–4 females, and 5–8 babies and young. They spend the day feeding and moving around, and at night they sleep in their nests.

Female gorillas groom each other's fur

Male silverback defends group

Young gorillas play

FACIAL EXPRESSIONS
Chimps, like many other monkeys and apes, tell other group members about their moods and intentions by body postures, sounds, and facial expressions—just like people.

Worried	Playful	Afraid	Excited

DEFENDING THE FAMILY
The chief male gorilla is a huge animal, twice as heavy as a man and much stronger. He protects the group from leopards and other predators by roaring, thrashing bushes, beating his chest, and charging in the undergrowth.

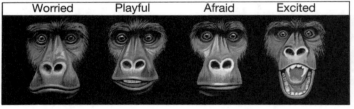

Lone male

- ■ Mature male
- ■ Mature female
- ■ Young male
- ■ Young female
- ■ Baby

Matriarch

Bachelor herd

Older male

HERD ON THE MOVE
The matriarch leads this extended elephant family. A group of young males comes near but then moves away. An older male walks nearby.

THE ELEPHANT HERD
Unlike gorillas, the elephant herd has a female in charge, the matriarch. She is older than the other 2–5 females in the herd. All adult females live with their offspring; young adult males form bachelor herds. Older males roam on their own and meet the females only at mating time.

THE DEFENSIVE GROUP

Musk oxen live on the cold, windswept lands of the far north. Their straggly fur is up to 24 inches long. One of their enemies is the wolf. Packs of wolves hang around the herd trying to pick off and eat the young, old, and sick oxen. Adult musk oxen protect their young and charge the wolves with lowered heads and sharp horns. A lone musk ox is an easy victim.

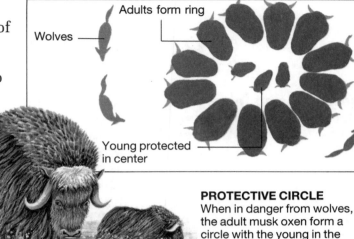

Wolves
Adults form ring
Young protected in center

PROTECTIVE CIRCLE
When in danger from wolves, the adult musk oxen form a circle with the young in the center, and face outward with their horns.

HUNTING IN GROUPS

In a group of African wild dogs, the adults help each other to catch and kill much larger animals, such as zebras and wildebeests. Such large quarry feeds the whole pack for several days. One or two pack leaders separate the victim from its herd, then the others join them to close in for the kill. The whole pack has a chance to feed on the prey.

African wild dog

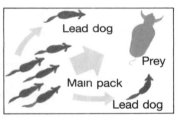

Lead dog
Prey
Main pack
Lead dog

THE CHASE
The prey tries to dodge and turn, but the two leading dogs cut the corners.

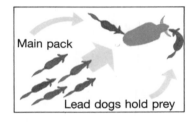

Main pack
Lead dogs hold prey

THE CAPTURE
One of the leading dogs grabs the prey's nose, and the other holds its rear end or tail.

Pack kills and eats prey

THE KILL
The rest of the pack rips out the soft rear belly to kill the prey and begin their meal.

GROUP SIGNALS

Madagascan lemurs communicate by sight and smell. Each lemur waves its striped tail, which has been smeared with its personal scent, like a "smelly flag."

Tail sends visual and scent signals

HELPING A GROUP MEMBER

Dolphins are intelligent, air-breathing mammals. They live in schools made up of loose, family groups. A sick dolphin could sink and drown. So others in its group may gather around and gently prod it upward. They help keep it near the surface, so that it can breathe until it recovers.

ORDER IN THE GROUP

In social animals, most group members get along with each other most of the time. Occasionally, disputes break out. Who has first pickings of a new food source? Who mates with whom at breeding time? In some social groups, there is a system of ranks called a dominance hierarchy. Dominant animals at the top of the hierarchy have first choice, especially of mates. This system stops wasteful fighting and helps group survival. As the top-ranking animals grow old, stronger and fitter challengers may take over.

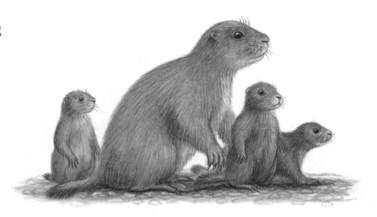

THE RUTTING SEASON

As the breeding season approaches, red deer stags (adult males) try to gather as many hinds (females) as possible, into a group called a harem. They roar at other stags, challenge them for extra hinds, and keep them away from their own harem. This time is known as the rut.

SPARRING STAGS

As two stags approach, they roar and face each other, heads lowered (1). Then they may walk parallel to each other, assessing the rival's size and fitness (2). Finally they may clash antlers, push, and wrestle in a trial of strength (3). Usually the biggest, strongest stags mate with the most females.

1 Facing   2 Assessing   3 Clashing

BODY LANGUAGE

Animals from insects to mammals communicate with others of their kind by the position of their head, body, and limbs. This body language helps keep order without actual fights and risk of injury. Wolves have many body signals, as do chimps (page 84).

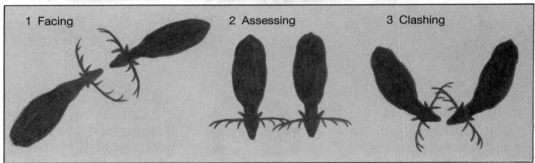

Nonaggressive   Submissive   Playful   Ready to attack   Ready to defend   Ready to attack or defend

THE PECKING ORDER

Dominance hierarchies are sometimes called "pecking orders" because they were first studied in farmyard chickens. The dominant or highest-ranking chicken can peck at all the others, to take over the best food or resting place. The second-ranking chicken can peck all the others except for the dominant one, and so on down the order.

1 Dominant

2

3

4 Subordinate

Dominant female

Young female

Young male challenger befriends females

Male

BABOON GROUPS

The baboon troop has a complicated hierarchy based on a senior female and her young, and her grown-up daughters and their babies. Males tend to come and go between troops. A male newcomer befriends females and challenges other males to establish a dominant position in the group. There may be 150 baboons in a big troop.

ELEPHANT SEAL BATTLES

The enormous elephant seals of the Pacific and Antarctic come ashore to their breeding beaches and fight aggressively for females. Unusual for the animal world, these fights may cause severe wounds, even death. The dominant alpha male, the "beachmaster," can mate with over 100 females.

GROOMING

When scientists study group behavior, especially in monkeys and apes, they note the order in which members groom each other to remove dirt and small pests from the fur. A dominant animal is groomed by a subordinate one first. Then, in return, the dominant one may groom the subordinate animal—or may not!

Chimps engaged in mutual grooming

CARE OF THE YOUNG

In a social group, new babies and playful youngsters are usually tolerated by their parents and other group members. Crocodile mothers were once thought to eat to eat their young as they hatched! It is now known that the mother gently carries her babies to water in her mouth; she looks after them for several weeks.

Male lion tolerates playful cub

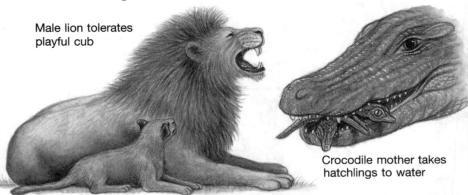

Crocodile mother takes hatchlings to water

GROUP ARCHITECTURE

Survival, particularly at breeding time, is often helped by a safe place to hide and rest. Small, solitary creatures like cockroaches can use a convenient crack. Numerous other animals actively build or dig some kind of shelter or nest. By cooperating in a large group, even tiny animals can build bigger, stronger homes for living and breeding. Weaver ants stitch leaves together, termites make earthen mounds, and wasps fashion paper domes. Group survival is the ultimate goal of this cooperative behavior.

BREEDING NESTS
Insects, fish, birds, and mammals are among the main nest-builders or nest-burrowers. A nest helps to keep young safe from predators and bad weather conditions. Birds' nests vary from a simple scrape in the soil and vegetation, as made by a red grouse, to an eagle's stick-and-twig aerie, which measures over ten feet across. When a bird or mammal species nests in a colony, or large group, many parents can work together to keep watch for predators and fight them off.

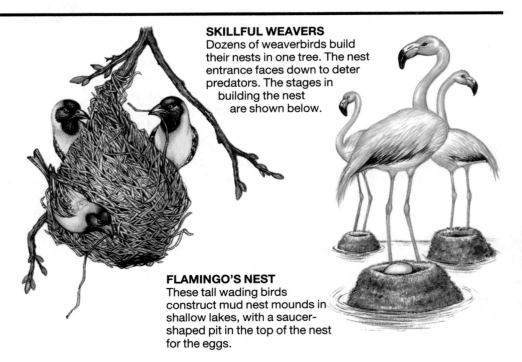

SKILLFUL WEAVERS
Dozens of weaverbirds build their nests in one tree. The nest entrance faces down to deter predators. The stages in building the nest are shown below.

FLAMINGO'S NEST
These tall wading birds construct mud nest mounds in shallow lakes, with a saucer-shaped pit in the top of the nest for the eggs.

WEAVING A NEST
A male weaverbird starts his intricate nest by using grass or palm-frond strips to make a loop (1). Then he adds more strips (2) and soon weaves a hollow nest ball (3, 4).

PARADISE FISH'S NEST
This tropical fish is a bubble-nest breeder. The eggs develop hidden in a floating mass of bubbles made by the male.

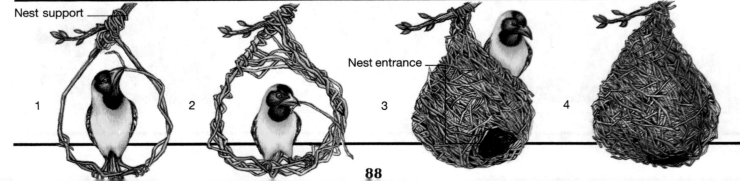

Nest support

Nest entrance

1   2   3   4

THE BEAVER'S FAMILY HOME

A beaver family—usually a male, female and several young—builds a dam of sticks, stones and mud across a stream. The dammed water forms a large pool in which the beavers construct their lodge, or house. It has an underwater entrance, a living chamber inside, and strong walls of branches and mud to keep out any predators who manage to get across the water. The beavers eat leaves and bark, and they store food in the pool.

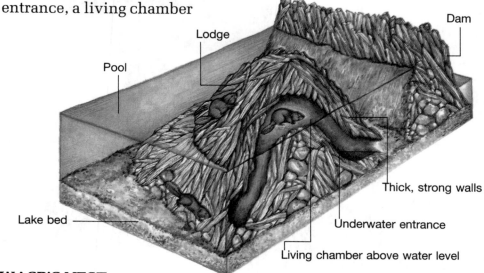

Dam

Lodge

Pool

Thick, strong walls

Underwater entrance

Lake bed

Living chamber above water level

WASP'S NEST

The "paper" of the common wasp's nest is made out of wood. The wasps scrape up the wood, chew it with saliva into a paste, and spread it out to dry to form the nest walls and the cells within.

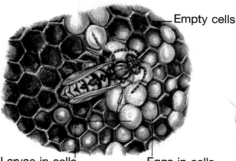

Empty cells

Larvae in cells

Eggs in cells

TERMITE'S NEST

The main living chambers in a termite nest are below ground, where it is cool, dark, and damp. The hard, dried-mud walls protect the inhabitants, and the tall "chimney" helps with cooling and air-conditioning. Workers continually mend and maintain the nest.

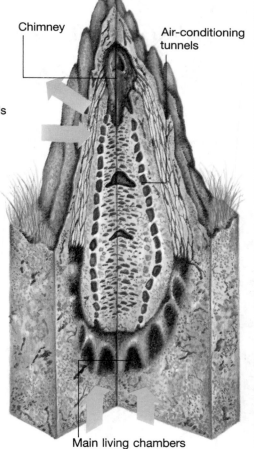

Chimney

Air-conditioning tunnels

Main living chambers

BUILDING MATERIALS

A bowl-shaped nest made by a wagtail, blackbird, or thrush contains a number of different building materials. The framework is usually twigs and thick grass stems. This is lined with thinner grass stems, scraps of moss, hair and fur, small feathers and leaves, and even human-made items such as string or paper. Some birds even pluck their own feathers to make a soft nest lining.

Wagtail's nest

Cattle hair

Lichen

String

Wood

Feathers

Grass

Moss

THE BIGGEST HOME

Australia's Great Barrier Reef is the largest animal-made structure on Earth. Millions of coral polyps, tiny anemone-like creatures that make stony walls around their soft bodies, have built up the reef over thousands of years.

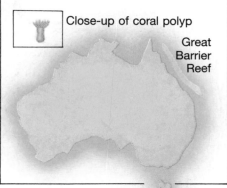

Close-up of coral polyp

Great Barrier Reef

HERDS, SWARMS, AND SCHOOLS

Some of nature's most impressive sights are huge herds of large mammals on the African plains, vast flocks of birds wheeling through the sky, and great schools of fish twisting and turning in the oceans. The social behavior of these group members and the ways they interact with each other are not as complicated as in a gorilla troop. These types of animals live together mainly because they find safety in numbers. Sometimes animals of very different species find benefits in living together.

CONFUSING A PREDATOR

While zebra feed together, there are usually one or two looking up, sniffing the air and listening for danger. When the watchers become alarmed, their escape reactions warn the rest of the herd. Thus the whole herd benefits from this continual lookout system. Also, a large mass of animals moving around makes it difficult for a predator to single out one victim.

TUNA SCHOOL
Dim shapes moving in the water, and the flashes and glints of light from the scales, make the school an awkward, shifting target for a predator such as a shark.

ZEBRA HERD
One theory behind why zebras have stripes is that when the herd panics, the stripes of individual animals merge and combine to "dazzle" and confuse a predator.

LIVING TOGETHER
Two different organisms living in a partnership that helps both is called symbiosis. A hermit crab is protected by a stinging anemone on its shell. The anemone eats scraps from the crab's meals.

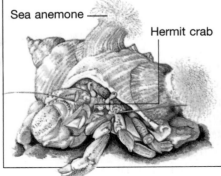

Sea anemone —

Hermit crab

SCHOOLING BEHAVIOR

Fish in a large school swim and dart with amazing synchronized precision, moving quickly yet staying the same distances apart. Their lateral lines (page 59) help in this coordinated movement. It is thought that predators see the resulting movement of the school as if it were one huge animal which would be too big to attack or eat.

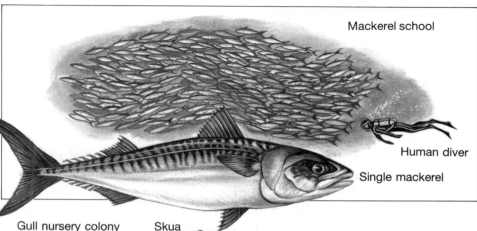

Mackerel school

Human diver

Single mackerel

Birds search at random

One finds food

Others crowd around

Gull nursery colony   Skua

BREEDING IN NUMBERS

A gull breeding colony is a mass of squawking chicks and busy parents. When a predator such as a skua comes near, many parent gulls fly at it and try to chase it away. One or two gull parents would have less chance of defending their eggs and chicks in this way. Foxes, snakes, and other hunters are similarly repelled.

FEEDING FLOCKS

Being in a large group can help at feeding time, as many eyes, ears, and noses search for food. A flock of starlings spreads out to feed. Each keeps an occasional watch on the others. When one finds food, the others notice and gather round to share the meal.

LIVING NEAR FOOD

Fanworms live protected in tubes half-buried in mud on the sea bottom. They filter tiny bits of floating food from the water with their delicate tentacles. Where the sea bed is suitably muddy, and a current brings plenty of food, the worms live and prosper.

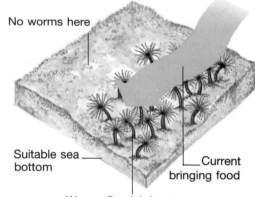

No worms here

Suitable sea bottom

Current bringing food

Worms flourish here

BREEDING SWARMS

In a flourishing ants' nest the population gradually rises. When it reaches a certain size, or at a specific time of year, some grubs develop into winged females and males. These fly off to begin new colonies.

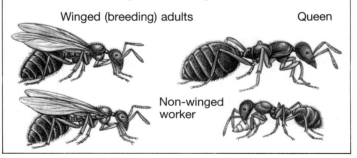

Winged (breeding) adults   Queen

Non-winged worker

GATHERING IN SWARMS

When their numbers are low, locusts have a mainly green coloration and live alone. As their numbers rise, the young locusts develop browner colors and gather in swarms, ready to devastate the countryside.

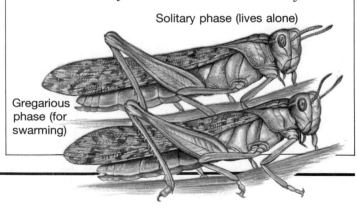

Solitary phase (lives alone)

Gregarious phase (for swarming)

THE WEB OF NATURE

Biologists nowadays have a reasonable idea of how most organisms work—how they feed, excrete, reproduce, and carry out the other processes of life. But living organisms do not exist in isolation. They are linked to each other by a vast network of relationships, such as who feeds on whom. An ecosystem is a community of plants, animals, and other organisms interacting with each other and the environment in which they live. Ecology is the study of all of these relationships.

Each kind of environment, such as a desert, is called a habitat. Within the habitat grow characteristic kinds of plants, like heather on the heathland, and grasses on the grassland. The plants provide the basic food (nutrients and energy) for the animals. Habitats, too, do not exist in isolation. They interconnect to form the gigantic web of life on Earth.

ENERGY FLOW

One way of studying an ecosystem is to look at the flow of energy through it. Plants capture the sun's energy (page 28) and use it for living. Herbivorous animals obtain some of this energy by eating the plants. Herbivores are then eaten by carnivores and so on. Detritivores feed on waste matter, so they recycle energy.

COLOR KEY

| Plants |
| Herbivores |
| Carnivores |
| Top carnivores |
| Detritivores |

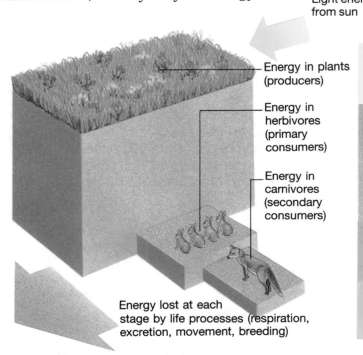

Light energy from sun

Energy in plants (producers)

Energy in herbivores (primary consumers)

Energy in carnivores (secondary consumers)

Energy lost at each stage by life processes (respiration, excretion, movement, breeding)

Elodea waterweed

Caddis fly larva

Stickleback

Great diving beetle

Bloodworm

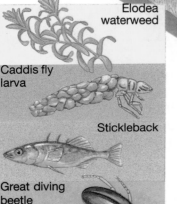

PONDS

Most ponds are shallow enough to have rooted plants in the deeper parts, as well as vegetation around the edges. Some nutrients are washed in by rain. Animals such as frogs and beetles come and go at different times of year.

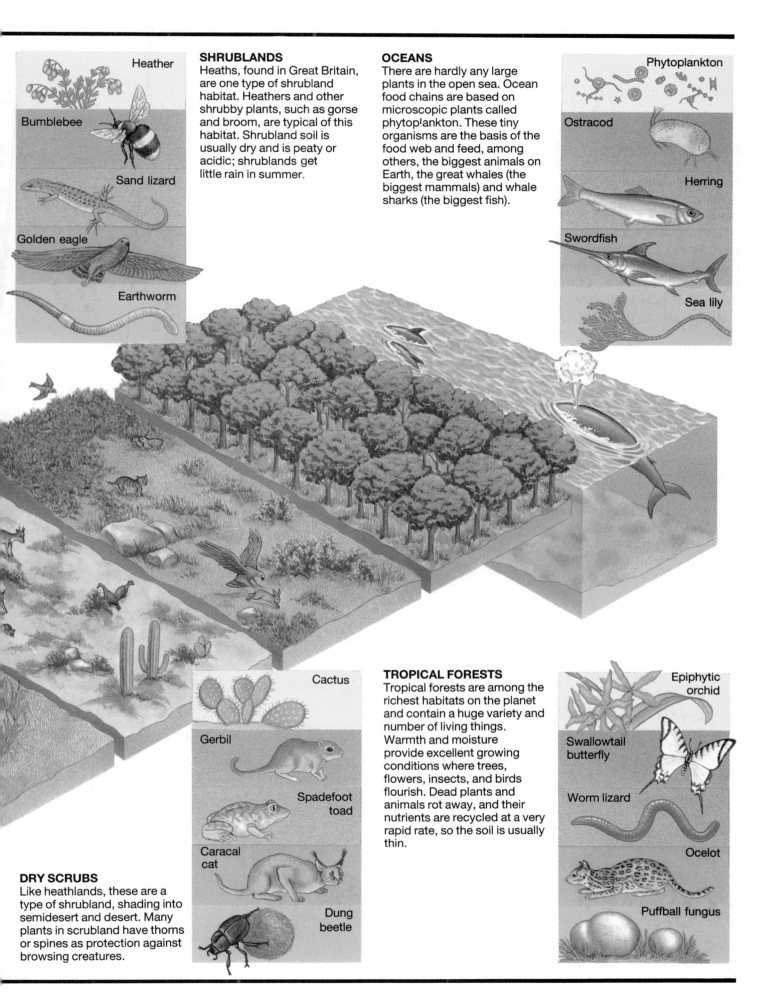

Heather

Bumblebee

Sand lizard

Golden eagle

Earthworm

SHRUBLANDS
Heaths, found in Great Britain, are one type of shrubland habitat. Heathers and other shrubby plants, such as gorse and broom, are typical of this habitat. Shrubland soil is usually dry and is peaty or acidic; shrublands get little rain in summer.

OCEANS
There are hardly any large plants in the open sea. Ocean food chains are based on microscopic plants called phytoplankton. These tiny organisms are the basis of the food web and feed, among others, the biggest animals on Earth, the great whales (the biggest mammals) and whale sharks (the biggest fish).

Phytoplankton

Ostracod

Herring

Swordfish

Sea lily

Cactus

Gerbil

Spadefoot toad

Caracal cat

Dung beetle

DRY SCRUBS
Like heathlands, these are a type of shrubland, shading into semidesert and desert. Many plants in scrubland have thorns or spines as protection against browsing creatures.

TROPICAL FORESTS
Tropical forests are among the richest habitats on the planet and contain a huge variety and number of living things. Warmth and moisture provide excellent growing conditions where trees, flowers, insects, and birds flourish. Dead plants and animals rot away, and their nutrients are recycled at a very rapid rate, so the soil is usually thin.

Epiphytic orchid

Swallowtail butterfly

Worm lizard

Ocelot

Puffball fungus

ATTACK AND DEFENSE

Nature is not always "red in tooth and claw," with continuous battles for survival between predators and prey. For long periods of time, animals go about their everyday business undisturbed. But when the hunt is on, things often happen very quickly. Predatory animals may attack with a cunning ambush, or with a full-frontal assault using speed and strength. The prey must respond at once, by rapidly escaping or with effective defense measures. Otherwise it will end up as yet another link in the food web.

DEFENSE STRATEGIES

Over millions of years, different organisms have evolved a huge variety of methods for defending themselves against predators. One form of defense is attack—to challenge the predator and fight back. Only bigger, well-armed prey animals are able to do this. Chemical weapons such as stings and poisonous bites can be very effective, and animals that have this type of defense are often brightly colored, as a warning to the would-be attacker. Predators learn to recognize these warning colors.

WEAPONS

Teeth are very hard and strong for biting and chewing. Extra-large teeth, like the boar's tusks, are a fearsome slashing defensive weapon.

Stinging chemical inside

Hair breaks easily

CHEMICALS

Certain plants have tiny hairs that break off easily and release irritating chemicals.

Boar defends with sharp tusks

Wolf attacks with canine teeth

Lizard erects large frills of skin

PLAYING DEAD

A hognose snake flops down "dead" when threatened. This act confuses some predators, who then give up the hunt.

Snake fakes death

Armadillo rolls into defensive ball

ROLLING UP

If in danger an armadillo, a pangolin, a hedgehog, and even a pillbug will roll into a well-protected ball.

RUNNING AWAY

The cheetah is fast but lacks stamina. If it does not catch an antelope on the first sprint, it gives up the chase.

Antelope zigzags to lose attacker

LOOKING BIGGER

Numerous creatures can puff up or make themselves look bigger when attacked. The Australian frilled lizard is well equipped for this.

CAMOUFLAGE

One way to avoid being attacked is to avoid being detected in the first place. Creatures who blend in with their surroundings, so that it is difficult to spot them, are said to be camouflaged. Camouflage involves colors and patterns, the overall shape of an animal, and its behavior. Some creatures, when camouflaged as leaves, sway in the breeze to look more realistic.

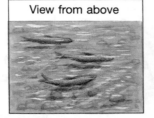
View from above

View from below

Darker back matches gloom of deeper water

Lighter underside matches surface glints

COUNTERSHADING

Some fish are darker on top and silvery below to match the surroundings when seen from above or beneath.

Leafy sea dragon

Leaf cricket

BODY SHAPES

The leafy sea dragon, a type of seahorse, blends in with swaying weeds. Some insects closely resemble leaves.

Green tree frog

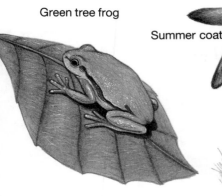

Summer coat

Winter coat

Fallow deer blends in with woodland

COLOR

A green tree frog chooses to sit on a green leaf. It would be obvious on brown bark. This is an example of the importance of behavior in camouflage.

CHANGING COLORS

The mountain hare has a brown summer coat. In autumn it molts the brown hairs and grows white fur for camouflage in snow and ice.

PATTERNS

The patchy coloration of some deer makes them almost invisible in the dappled woodland shade—provided they keep still.

DANGER COLORS

Yellow and black or red and black are common warning colors in nature. Bees, wasps, hornets, poison frogs, snakes, and even distasteful salamanders have them to warn off enemies.

MIMICRY

In nature a mimic is a harmless organism that is shaped and colored to resemble a harmful one. The warning colors of harmful animals advertise that they are dangerous, and predators soon learn to leave them alone. So these predators also avoid the similarly colored mimics. Mimicry is also employed by some flowers to attract bees and other animals to carry their pollen.

King snake

Coral snake

BEE OR FLOWER?

Mimicry does not occur only for reasons of defense. The bee orchid mimics a bee. A real bee tries to mate with the flower but gets a blob of pollen instead, which it then transfers to another orchid to pollinate it.

Bumble bee

Bee orchid

FLY OR WASP?

The hoverfly is harmless but resembles the wasp, which has a painful sting.

Wasp

Hoverfly

Emperor moth

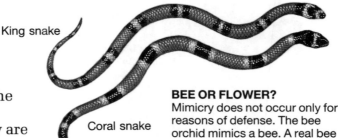

CAT OR HAWK—OR MIMIC?

Moths such as the emperor, and butterflies like the peacock, have large "eyespots" on their wings. When these are suddenly exposed they may scare away a predator by their resemblance to the eyes of an owl, hawk, or cat.

95

PREDATORS AND PREY

A powerful airborne hunter, the golden eagle, swoops over a rocky mountainside and grasps a marmot in its talons. The capture means one less prey and one well-fed predator. But why don't eagles and other predators breed and multiply and ultimately kill all the marmots and other prey? One reason is that a too-successful predator would eventually destroy its own food source. In general, a long-term balance between predators and prey is maintained, although populations often change through time.

POPULATION CYCLES

The numbers of certain animals fluctuate, building to a peak over several years then falling. If such a population cycle involves preyed-upon animals, such as lemmings or rabbits, the numbers of their predators may also increase and decrease, lagging slightly behind the prey.

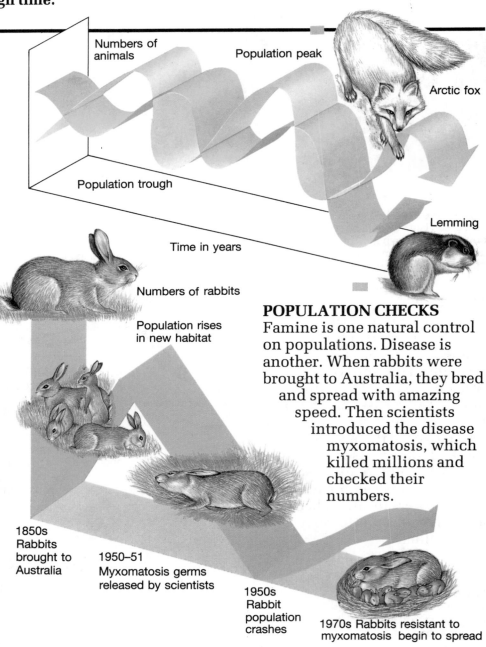

Numbers of animals

Population peak

Arctic fox

Population trough

Time in years

Lemming

Numbers of rabbits

POPULATION EXPLOSIONS

When food is plentiful, lemming numbers boom. The area gets crowded and food runs short. The lemmings set off to find new food. Many are killed by predators or may die by drowning in rivers, falling from cliffs, or starving.

Population rises in new habitat

POPULATION CHECKS

Famine is one natural control on populations. Disease is another. When rabbits were brought to Australia, they bred and spread with amazing speed. Then scientists introduced the disease myxomatosis, which killed millions and checked their numbers.

Lemmings fall off cliffs

1850s Rabbits brought to Australia

1950–51 Myxomatosis germs released by scientists

1950s Rabbit population crashes

1970s Rabbits resistant to myxomatosis begin to spread

THE ETOSHA STORY

The intricate links between living things and their surroundings, and how these can be upset by human interference, were shown by events in Etosha National Park, in southern Africa. The disturbances began when gravel was dug from areas in the park for road building. Among the many effects were fewer zebras and wildebeest, and more lions. These changes had many more unforeseen consequences in the area.

1 Gravel is dug out, leaving pits. Pits fill with stagnant water.

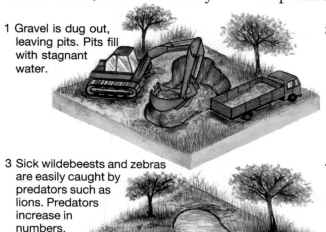

2 Anthrax germs thrive in stagnant water. Germs taken in by drinking animals such as wildebeests and zebras.

3 Sick wildebeests and zebras are easily caught by predators such as lions. Predators increase in numbers.

4 Predators run out of zebras and wildebeests. Predators hunt eland, which are resistant to anthrax. Eland numbers fall.

BREEDING CYCLES

When elephant numbers are low and conditions are good, females usually give birth to a calf every three or four years. If conditions deteriorate, or if the numbers rise and the elephants become crowded, the time between calf births becomes longer. This helps to stabilize the population.

Most female elephants are able to breed by 10–15 years of age. They have most calves between the ages of 25 and 45. Few female elephants over the age of 50 are able to breed. The pregnancy of an elephant lasts 18–22 months—the longest of any mammal.

THE KAIBAB STORY

This is an example of how human activities can have unforeseen effects on the delicate balance between predators and prey. On Kaibab plateau in Arizona, changes occurred when people began to hunt coyotes and pumas, which preyed upon the local deer population.

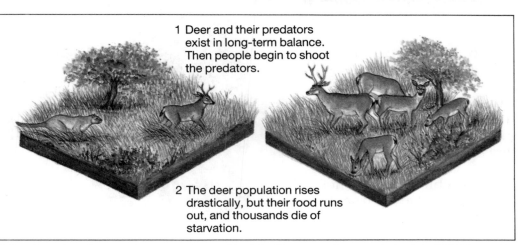

1 Deer and their predators exist in long-term balance. Then people begin to shoot the predators.

2 The deer population rises drastically, but their food runs out, and thousands die of starvation.

GLOSSARY

The following descriptions aim to explain, in a simple way, words and terms as they are used in this book. Some of the terms have more restricted scientific meanings or wider everyday usages. Consult a good dictionary for these. Words in *italics* have their own entries in the Glossary.

Aerobe A living thing that needs a continuous supply of oxygen to survive. Compare *anaerobe*.

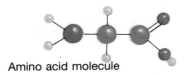
Amino acid molecule

Amino acid A type of smallish *molecule* containing the carboxyl (-COOH) and amino (-NH₂) chemical groupings. About 20 common amino acids constitute the building blocks of *proteins* in living things.

Anaerobe A living thing that can exist without oxygen. There are far fewer anaerobes (chiefly certain bacteria) than *aerobes*.

Animal A member of one of the major groups (kingdoms) of living things. Animals feed by eating and digesting other life forms and absorbing the nutrients.

Aquatic Found always or mostly in water. Fish, whales, diving beetles, and jellyfish are all aquatic animals.

Artery A blood vessel that carries blood away from the heart.

Atmosphere The layer of gases and vapors above the surface of the Earth, which becomes progressively less dense at greater distances from the Earth. It consists mainly of nitrogen (four-fifths) and oxygen (one-fifth).

Atom The smallest part of an *element* that still has the physical and chemical properties of that element and can take part in a chemical reaction; the smallest part of an element, which cannot be subdivided under ordinary conditions.

Axon The long, thin, wire-shaped part of a *neuron* (nerve cell).

Bacteria Microscopic single-celled life forms belonging to the *moneran group*. They have no *cell nucleus*, they live almost everywhere, and some cause diseases, such as pneumonia, in other living things.

Biochemical Referring to chemical events and reactions that occur in a living thing.

Biology The scientific study of life and living things. It includes the study of animals (zoology), animal behavior (ethology), plants (botany or plant biology), cells (cytology), how genes are passed on from one generation to the next (genetics), the relationships between living things and their environment (ecology), and other specialist areas.

Biosphere The thin "layer of life" at, just beneath, and above the Earth's surface, where living things can exist.

Blue-green algae Simple one-celled living things, which lack a proper cell *nucleus*, and which are usually classified as *monerans*. They are not true plants, but they can capture light energy by *photosynthesis*. Also called *cyanobacteria*.

Botany See *biology*.

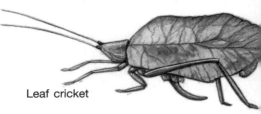
Leaf cricket

Camouflage Blending in with the surroundings to avoid detection.

Capillary A blood vessel with walls only one or a few cells thick. Oxygen and nutrients pass from the blood through the capillary wall to the body parts beyond. Carbon dioxide and other wastes pass from the body parts through the capillary wall into the blood, to be taken away for disposal.

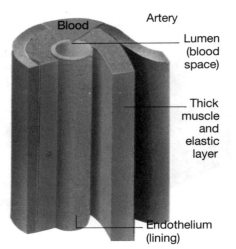
Artery
Blood
Lumen (blood space)
Thick muscle and elastic layer
Endothelium (lining)

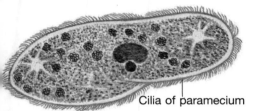
Cilia of paramecium

Carbohydrate A type of *molecule* containing atoms of carbon, hydrogen and oxygen. Examples are sugars, starches, and *cellulose*.

Carnivore An animal that feeds mainly on the flesh of other animals.

Cell The smallest component of a living thing; the basic unit of life. Some life forms consist of a single cell, such as *bacteria* and *protists*. Others, like the human body, are made of billions of cells.

Cell membrane See *membrane*.

Cellular respiration See *respiration*.

Cellulose A type of *carbohydrate* molecule which forms the basic structural material in plants, especially the wall of a plant *cell*.

Chlorophyll A special type of molecule, found only in plants and some protists, which can capture light energy and convert it into chemical energy, by the process of *photosynthesis*. Chlorophyll is usually green.

Chloroplasts Tiny green structures inside plant cells (especially in the leaves). They contain *chlorophyll* and capture light energy by the process of *photosynthesis*.

Chromosomes The thread-like structures inside a *cell* which contain the genetic material, in the form of *DNA*.

Cilia Microscopic hairs projecting from the surface of a *cell*. They usually flick back and forth with an oar-like motion.

Circulation The system whereby nutrients and oxygen are spread to all parts of the body, and/or wastes are collected for removal. This is usually achieved by a fluid, such as blood, which is pumped around the body by an *organ* such as the heart.

Consumer An organism that takes in ready-made, energy-containing nutrients. Compare *producers*.

Convergent evolution When the bodies of living things come to look alike because they are adapted for the same way of life. It can also apply to body parts which do a similar job. See also *evolution*.

Crop Part of the *gut* of animals, such as birds, usually

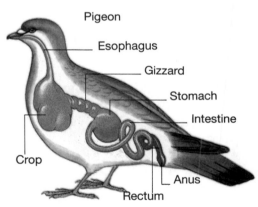
Pigeon
Esophagus
Gizzard
Stomach
Intestine
Crop
Anus
Rectum

specialized for storing food before it can be digested.

Cyanobacteria See *blue-green algae*.

Cytology See *biology*.

Cytoplasm The watery-looking fluid inside a cell, in which are found the various cell *organelles*. In fact, cytoplasm is not a "disorganized soup," it is highly structured with channels and definite regions.

Detritivore A living thing that feeds on the dying, dead, or rotting remains of plants, animals, and other life forms.

DNA double helix
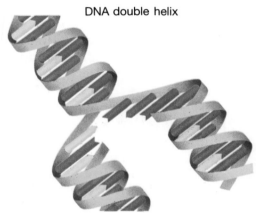

DNA Deoxyribonucleic acid, the substance that forms the inherited material or genes, which are passed from one generation to the next. It is found mainly in a cell's *nucleus* in the form of *chromosomes*, and also in *mitochondria*. See also *genetics*.

Dominance hierarchy A system of ranks for *social* animals, in which one or a few animals in the group are "in charge" and have first choice over the other, subordinate, members.

Ecology See *biology*.

Element In science, a substance consisting of identical *atoms*; a substance that cannot be split into constituent substances. Carbon, oxygen, nitrogen, iron, and aluminum are all elements.

Endoplasmic reticulum (ER) A *membrane system inside a cell*, which may or may not be studded with *ribosomes*. The ER is concerned mainly with making, moving, and storing *cell* products such as *proteins*.

Enzyme A type of *molecule* that speeds up or slows down a *biochemical* reaction in a living thing. Enzymes are mostly *proteins,* and they control and coordinate the complex chemistry inside the body's cells, digest food, and carry out many other functions.

Esophagus Part of the *gut* of an animal, usually long and tube-shaped, which conveys swallowed food from the mouth to the *stomach*.

Ethology The study of animal behavior. See also *biology*.

Evolution The continuing process of change in the natural world, as shown by the evidence of *fossils*. As conditions and environments alter, living things gradually change to become better suited, or adapted, to surviving. Those which cannot adapt may die out completely (see *extinct*).

Extant When a *species* or larger group of living things

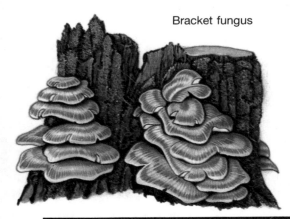

Bracket fungus

still survives and lives on Earth. Compare *extinct.*

Extinct When a *species* or larger group of living things has disappeared and died out completely. Compare *extant.*

Excretion The process of getting rid of waste products from the body of a living thing. In animals such as mammals and birds, the main *organs* involved in excretion are the kidneys.

Fats Types of, and a common name for, *lipids*. The term is also used to describe substances found in the bodies of certain animals, which act as an energy supply, insulator, and shock absorber.

Food chain A series of feeding relationships in which an *herbivore* eats a *plant*, and is then eaten by a *carnivore* or *detritivore*, and so on. Most food chain diagrams depict only the main food items of the animals concerned, since in the real world the different feeding links are usually very complicated. See also *food web*.

Food web An interlinked series of *food chains*, that builds up to give an overall picture of the feeding relationships in an area or *habitat*.

Fossil The marks or remains of a once-living organism, such as a plant or animal, which have been preserved in rocks or other substances. Fossils play an important part in the study of *evolution*.

Fungi One of the major groups (kingdoms) of living things.

They obtain energy by breaking down and rotting away the bodies of other living things and absorbing the nutrients into their own bodies. Mushrooms, toadstools, yeasts, mildews, and slime molds are all types of fungi.

Gas-exchange respiration See *respiration.*

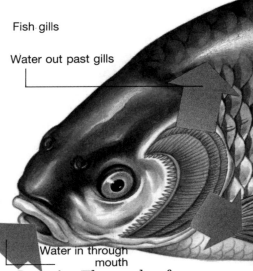

Fish gills

Water out past gills

Water in through mouth

Genetics The study of genes and DNA, and how features are passed on (inherited) from one generation of living things to the next. See also *biology.*

Gill A body part specialized for absorbing oxygen from water, as in fishes, sea slugs, and various other *aquatic* creatures.

Golgi body A stacking system of *membranes* inside a cell, which is usually involved in packaging, storing, and exporting cell products.

Gut A general term for the digestive tube in an animal, in which food is broken down into small molecules and absorbed into the body. Parts of the gut include the crop, stomach, and intestine.

Habitat A type of living place characterized by a certain kind of plant and animal community, such as oak woodland, rocky seashore, heathland, or riverbank.

Herbivore An animal that eats mainly plant matter such as leaves, shoots, or flowers.

Host In biology, a living thing from which a *parasite* obtains its food, shelter, or both.

Intestine Part of the *gut* of an animal, specialized for food breakdown (by *enzymes*) and absorption.

Invertebrate An animal without a backbone. Major invertebrate groups include worms, insects, spiders, and mollusks. Compare *vertebrate*.

Lateral line A *sense organ* along the side of a fish's body, which detects water movements and vibrations.

Leucoplast A structure inside a plant cell, which usually stores energy reserves such as *lipids* or *carbohydrates*.

Life cycle The cycle of events in one complete generation of

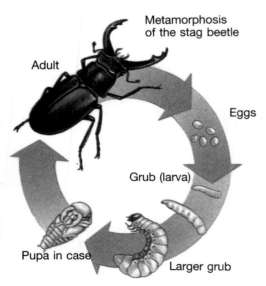

Metamorphosis of the stag beetle

Adult

Eggs

Grub (larva)

Pupa in case

Larger grub

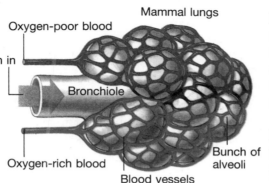

Mammal lungs

Oxygen-poor blood

Oxygen in

Bronchiole

Oxygen-rich blood

Bunch of alveoli

Blood vessels

a living thing. In the life cycle of a chicken, an adult chicken lays an egg, the egg hatches, and the chick grows into an adult.

Lipids A group of *molecules* found in living things, which are fatty, oily, or waxy. They contain mainly carbon and oxygen.

Lungs Body parts specialized for obtaining oxygen (and usually getting rid of carbon dioxide) in air-breathing animals.

Lysosomes Small structures inside cells that contain powerful chemicals such as digestive *enzymes*.

Malphigian tubules Long, thin tubes inside the bodies of insects and spiders, involved in *excretion*.

Meiosis A special type of cell division (or multiplication), in which a parent cell splits to produce four cells which each have only half the number of *chromosomes* of the parent cell. These offspring cells may be egg or sperm cells. Compare *mitosis*.

Membrane A layer, sheet, or film which separates one region from another. In living things, a membrane forms the "skin" around a *cell*.

Membranes also make up the outside boundaries of various structures inside the cell, such as *vacuoles*, *mitochondria*, the cell's *nucleus*, as well as *chloroplasts*.

Metamorphosis When a living thing changes its body shape and form drastically during its *life cycle*, as when a caterpillar changes into a chrysalis, or a tadpole changes into a frog.

Mimicry When one living thing is shaped, colored, and has other features in order to resemble, or mimic, another.

Mitochondria Small sausage-shaped structures inside cells,

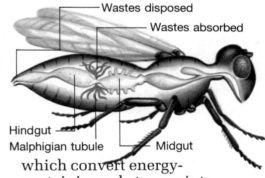

Wastes disposed

Wastes absorbed

Hindgut

Malphigian tubule

Midgut

which convert energy-containing substances into energy-rich molecules more easily used by the cell's *biochemical* machinery.

Mitosis The "normal" type of division (or multiplication) of a cell, in which it splits to produce two daughter cells that are identical to it. Compare *meiosis*.

Molecule Two or more *atoms* joined together; the smallest portion of a substance capable of independent existence, which still has the properties of the original substance. Molecules of oxygen gas each have two atoms of oxygen (O_2). Each molecule of water has two hydrogen atoms and one oxygen atom (H_2O).

Moneran A member of one of the major groups (kingdoms) of living things, Monera. A moneran is a single-celled life form which does not have a proper *membrane*-bound nucleus inside the cell. The group includes *bacteria* and *blue-green algae*.

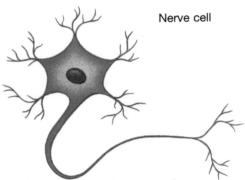

Nerve cell

Motor nerve A *nerve* that transmits nerve signals from the brain to a muscle, to make the animal move.

Natural Part of nature, unaffected or uninterfered with by people.

Nerve A bundle of *neurons*, and especially their wire-shaped *axons*. See also *sensory nerve, motor nerve, neuron*.

Neuron A nerve *cell*, specialized for conducting tiny electrical nerve signals along its wire-shaped *axon*.

Nucleus The control center of the *cell*, containing the *DNA* that makes up the genetic material passed from one generation to the next.

Omnivore An animal that eats both plant and animal matter.

Organ A main part of an animal's body, such as the brain, heart, or kidney.

Organelle A structure inside a *cell*, such as a *mitochondrion, chloroplast*, or *nucleus*.

Organism A living thing or life form, ranging from a microscopic germ to a giant tree or whale.

Parasite An organism that obtains food from another type of living thing (the host), usually by living in or on its body, and gives nothing in return. It may cause harm and sometimes death to the host.

Pheromone A smell or odor chemical produced by an animal, which is released into the surroundings, and which has an effect on the behavior of others of its kind.

Photosynthesis The *biochemical* process by which plants convert carbon dioxide and water into sugar. The word means "making with light," and the plants actually use energy from the sun's light to power the process.

Plant One of the major groups (kingdoms) of living things. Plants have cells with proper nuclei (see *nucleus*), and they capture light energy by the process of *photosynthesis*. Seaweeds, mosses, ferns, flowers, and trees are all plants.

Predator A hunting animal, a *carnivore*, which captures and eats another animal, known as the *prey*.

Prey See *predator*.

The golden eagle is a well-known predator

The cuckoo is a brood parasite

Producers Another term for *plants* and certain *monerans*, which produce all the energy-containing foods on which animals and other life forms depend. Compare *consumer*.

Protein A very important type of molecule, found only in living or once-living things. Most proteins are composed of strings of about 20 different kinds of *amino acids* joined together. Proteins are essential structural and functional molecules, forming hair, nails, skin, cellular parts such as *membranes*, and *enzymes*.

Protist A single-celled life form with a *nucleus*, including living things such as amoebas and algae (simple plants). In most classifications, Protista is one of the major groups (kingdoms) of living things. Protozoa and protophyta are included as protists.

Radula The rasplike or file-like "tongue," with tiny teeth, of slugs and snails.

Reflex A body movement or reaction that happens automatically, without the brain having to instruct the part to move. An example is when the eye blinks if something comes too near it.

Respiration The process of getting energy in a useable form out of energy-rich molecules. Cellular respiration includes the *biochemical* pathways inside a *cell* by which this happens, and it requires oxygen. The word "respiration" is sometimes used for the oxygen-obtaining process too, as in breathing. Gas-exchange respiration is the swopping of oxygen for the waste product carbon dioxide, in the lungs or similar organs.

Ribosomes Small buds or spheres inside a cell, which are the main producers of *proteins*. They may float in the cell or be attached to the *endoplasmic reticulum*.

Sense organ An *organ* that tells an animal about some aspect of the world around it, or about events inside its own body, and produces tiny electrical nerve signals as a result. For example, the sense organs of sight are the eyes.

Sensory nerve A *nerve* that transmits electrical nerve signals from a *sense organ* to the brain.

Social animal An animal that lives in a group, usually with others of its own kind, and that interacts and cooperates with group members.

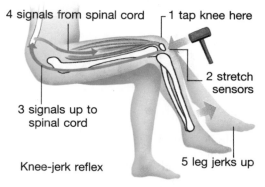

4 signals from spinal cord
1 tap knee here
2 stretch sensors
3 signals up to spinal cord
5 leg jerks up

Knee-jerk reflex

Species A basic grouping of living things that are similar to each other and can breed with each other to produce offspring which themselves can breed together. All lions belong to one species; tigers to another; and leopards to another. Each species has a unique international scientific name, usually in Latin or Greek, and usually printed in italics. The lion species is *Panthera leo*; tigers are *Panthera tigris*; leopards are *Panthera pardus*. All human beings belong to the species *Homo sapiens*.

Spore A usually microscopic structure produced by certain plants, fungi, and bacteria. A spore is often designed to withstand adverse conditions, and it grows into a new individual or into the next stage of the organism's *life cycle*.

Stomach Part of the *gut* of an animal, usually specialized for food storage and food breakdown by acids and *enzymes*.

Stomata Tiny holes or pores in the surface of a plant, usually in the "skin" of a leaf. They allow oxygen to enter and reach the cells within and carbon dioxide and excess water to pass out.

Thorax In an insect, the central section of the three-part body, which usually bears legs and wings. In a creature such as a bird or mammal, the thorax is another name for the chest, which contains the heart and lungs.

Tissue In a living thing, groups of similar *cells* with the same special features and jobs. Lots of muscle cells make up muscle tissue, which is specialized to contract.

Vacuole A *membrane*-bound bag, sac, or similar structure inside a cell. It usually stores substances such as digested food or cell products. Many plant cells have a large central vacuole, which is mostly water, that takes up nine-tenths of the total cell volume.

Vein A blood vessel that carries blood back to the heart.

Vertebrate An animal with a backbone. The main groups are fish, amphibians, reptiles, birds, and mammals. Compare *invertebrate*.

Zoology See *biology*.

Insect's eyes

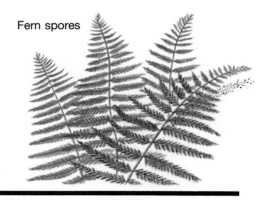

Fern spores

INDEX

ACKNOWLEDGMENTS

The publishers would like to thank the following artists
for contributing to this book:

Steve Weston (Linden Artists) 14–15; Craig Austin
1617, 22–23, 24–25, 26–27, 32–33, 34–35, 38–39,
40–41, 46–47, 54–55, 56–57, 64–65, 92–93,;
Neil Bulpitt 18–19; Oxford Illustrators 20–21, 44–45,
74–75, 76–77, 78–79, 80–81; Ray Grinaway (The Garden
Studio) 28–29, 58–59, 70–71, 82–83, 84–85;
Jim Channell 30–31, 62–63; Angela Hargreaves
36–37; Charlotte Kennedy (Jillian Burgess) 42–43;
Bernard Robinson 48–49, 50–51; Richard Combes 52–53;
Caroline Barnard 72–73; Graham Austen (The Garden
Studio) 60–61; Anne Winterbotham and Richard Draper
66–67, 68–69; Eva Mellhuish (The Garden Studio) 86–87,
94–95; Tracy Wayte (David Lewis Agency)
88–89, 90–91, 96–97; additional material –
Matthew Gore, Mark Franklin, Terence Lambert,
Alan Harris, John Davis and Doreen McGuiness